THE PHOENIX – RISING FROM THE ASHES

Faith is seeing light with your heart when all your
eyes see is darkness ahead. –unknown

DIAN GRIFFIN JACKSON

abbott press®

A DIVISION OF WRITER'S DIGEST

Scripture quotations marked are taken from the Holy Bible, New International Version®, NIV®. Copyright © 1973, 1978, 1984 by Biblica, Inc.™ Used by permission of Zondervan. All rights reserved worldwide. http://www.zondervan.com

This book is a work of fiction. Names, characters, places, and incidents are the product of the author's imagination or are used fictitiously. The events taking place in the story come from the imagination and life's experiences of the author. Events or situations as described in this book with reference to real locations, establishments, and actual persons are coincidental.

Abbott Press books may be ordered through booksellers or by contacting:

Abbott Press
1663 Liberty Drive
Bloomington, IN 47403
www.abbottpress.com
Phone: 1-866-697-5310

Because of the dynamic nature of the Internet, any web addresses or links contained in this book may have changed since publication and may no longer be valid. The views expressed in this work are solely those of the author and do not necessarily reflect the views of the publisher, and the publisher hereby disclaims any responsibility for them.

Any people depicted in stock imagery provided by Thinkstock are models, and such images are being used for illustrative purposes only. Certain stock imagery © Thinkstock.

ISBN: 978-1-4582-1527-7 (sc)
ISBN: 978-1-4582-1528-4 (e)

Library of Congress Control Number: 2014906473

Printed in the United States of America.

Abbott Press rev. date: 07/28/2014

DEDICATION AND ACKNOWLEDGEMENTS

I dedicate this book to the memory of my oldest son, Franciscus James Dixon, who was consistent and insistent that I step out of my comfort zone and become the next "Shirley Ceasar". We were talking about the movie, Fighting Temptations, when he said to me: "Mom, when are you going to be in the movies and tour around the world with your music and ministry? You remind me of Shirley Ceasar." Franciscus, you are not here to see your mother reach this most significant milestone in her life, completion of her first book; however, thoughts of you have been my inspiration and motivation, and your spiritual presence warms my heart. Thank you for believing in me and reaching beyond the grave to encourage me and live on in my life. I love you, ~ ***Mom***

I also acknowledge my daughter, Crystle Kidada Dixon, the one who holds my heart gently and with care, who read the entire book and provided many editorial comments that have made this book as successful as I know it will be. To my oldest living son, Dylan Adriece Jackson, whose enthusiastic support after reading the first draft of my book was so contagious I began to edit and rewrite in earnest. To Darian Alexander Jackson, the youngest, who did not read the book, preferring to wait until it was bound in its final cover, because, in his words "it makes me sad", but from whom I received lots of love and inspiration along the way. And to my nieta, Kymberli Cheyenne Smith, who at seven, read a few pages and helped Abuela in her own special way to finish telling the story.

I am grateful to all who have impacted my life or offered encouraging words throughout the incubation and birth of this work, and to you, I say thank you. The following persons were instrumental in reading and providing technical and material feedback and deserves worthy mention within these pages, including: my own personal editor, Dr. Carole Waterford Troxler, Professor Emeritus, Elon University; Dr. Nancy Ellet Allison, Pastor, Holy Covenant United Church of Christ; Gwendolyn Blue, CEO, WireCentric; Vickie Griffin Robertson, GAO and IG Program Analyst, Missile Defense Agency; and Dr. Earl Jerry Griffin, Pastor, Lane Chapel Christian Methodist Church, and Certified Speaker, Trainer, and Coach, John Maxwell Group. To each of you I express my deepest appreciation for your willingness and diligence in helping my dream come true. As you know, I have dreamed of being an author for many years. I am celebrating now because you did not give up on me.

To my parents, Earl and Nettie Mae Rogers Griffin, without whom there could not be a book written by this budding author. Thank you, Mom and Earl. You rock! It is my hope that you are proud of your middle daughter, and are rejoicing in the afterlife, knowing that she is doing well.

Finally, I am humbled and eternally grateful to the Creator of all, whom I know as God, who has endowed me with gifts, strength, and determination to rise above my circumstances and allow God to be glorified in my life. Indeed, I have lived amid the ashes of despair, yet, like the Phoenix, I rise.

FOREWORD ONE

"When a train goes through a tunnel and it gets dark,

you don't throw away the ticket and jump off.

You sit still and trust the engineer."

~ Corrie Ten Boom

Journeys take us away from something, through something, and to something. This novel depicts a journey of a traveler who left home in pain, lived with this pain through two abusive marriages, all the while being undervalued, marginalized, and underestimated in each relationship. Yet because of her inward strength, born from knowing deep in her heart that "greater was coming" she kept moving. She was constantly moving away from pain, through the darkness with an abiding faith in her that she could rise victorious as a conqueror. She refused to exist as a victim, rather with each step on her journey she has developed, grown, and fashioned her resolve to be that person she met as a little girl, adventurous, joyful, passionate, and alive. That image of herself allowed her to hold herself together until doors of opportunity opened for her to reach her destination. The journey is not over, the lessons learned are not final, but the path is clearer and brighter because she did not jump off the train, she trusted her inner conductor. This book will hold your imagination, your mind, and your attention to the very last word. I know the author personally; she is my sister and she is a phenomenal lady.

—Rev. Dr. Earl J. Griffiin

FOREWORD TWO

Every so often a book is written that challenges our thinking and questions long held teachings! This is that book. The author has crafted a masterpiece that will make one cry, laugh, shake one's head, and go ahhh. Melanie, university graduate, a devoted wife and mother, pastor, and many things in between, is in search of love and acceptance that has eluded her since birth. In Melanie's story is a child/woman who has lived her life believing she was out of God's favor only to find the exact opposite to be true. In therapy, she discovers there is a thirsty, hungry, needy little girl inside that is searching for her parents' love and acceptance. She is on a quest to find the man who will love her enough to help her right the wrongs both she and her mother experienced, and to reconcile the disenfranchised little girl with the beautiful, phenomenal woman she is certain the Creator has created her to be. Follow Melanie's struggles, from a child to maturity, and learn how Melanie's faith, trust, and belief in the God within her has sustained her through many obstacles, as she rises from the ashes of despair!

CONTENTS

God is a Doodle Bug!© - Dian Griffin Jackson, July 2007

I used to play with doodle bugs.

I was very young then.

It was summer.

Hot. Dry. Windless. Long days.

Bumble bees. Flies. Watermelon.

After all my chores were done

I'd go outside.

The day was still.

I'd go under our house.

But first, I'd find a small twig.

I would stir my twig in the dirt.

Under my house, over and over.

Stir. Stir. Stir.

I'd sing too of course.

I remember it well.

"Doodle bug, doodle bug, come get your coffee."

Didn't have any coffee, you know.

Wondered if the doodle bugs knew it.

Wondered if that's why it seemed to take hours before I finally stirred up a doodle bug.

Didn't mind at all.

You see, while I was stirring, waiting for the doodle bug,

Something beautiful would happen.

Another voice entered my consciousness.

Gentle. Soft. Playful. Sweet.

It was God, of course.

Couldn't tell anyone about that.

Couldn't tell anyone that God's voice did not sound like thunder.

Couldn't tell anyone that God spoke to me, played with me, laughed with me.

Couldn't tell anyone I thought God was a doodle bug.

PROLOG

If you've chosen this book, it's probably because the title grabbed your attention, or one of the reviewer's comments inspired you. You could be reading because you are convinced that something within these pages will resonate with your own story, or that of someone very close to you. I encourage you to keep reading. It gets better. Kinkier too! I've been taught to play the hand I've been dealt, and wait for my happiness in the sky. Truth is, this is anathema to what Jesus taught. I was playing Words with Friends with my brother and he and I hit on this conversation. Jesus taught us to "change those damning situations, relationships, and environments that prevent us from enjoying the abundant life," he said.

Total agreement. It takes work, perseverance, focus, and courage to challenge the teachings of the church that says one can't question God. Of course we can question God! Malachi 3:10: Try me. Prove me. Test me. If we can prove God in terms of finances, it goes without saying we can ask God about anything, even politics. I contend the reason we have that misconception in the church is because a man devised it as a way of keeping others (women and children) from questioning him [not God]. After all, if there is such a God, surely our little questions won't make this God mad! On the contrary.

On the other hand, if men could convince the church that he was the only species created in God's image, then of course, [h]e is most like God, right? And his authority becomes power. Who wants to abdicate power? Poppycock. Question God. Ask God.

Unlike man, God wants us to seek truth and knowledge. It's called a brain. How does one seek without asking! Knock and the door will be opened; enlightenment will come. Ask and you will find answers. Seek and you will find solutions. Use your brain. Light bulb! God does not seek to be master and lord of our lives—we have made God into that. Jesus said to his followers, "I no longer call you servant, I call you friend." Jesus asked. Are you sure you want me to drink this cup, God? Did you send me for other than the children of Israel, God? Are the laws and commandments of the prophets intended to be constrictive, or is there a better way, God? Jesus asked God questions during his entire recorded earthly sojourn. Surely we who are his followers, also can ask.

Throughout the centuries, beginning with the first book of the Bible in 1000-800 BCE, men have claimed an authority and sense of entitlement over women and children, that have assured their role of male dominance in every aspect of societal living. Alas! I've discovered that women have been brainwashed and scripturally hijacked so soundly, we are culpable in maintaining the status quo. We succumb to the myth that God's will (who of course is unquestionably male) for women is to put up with the crap we are saddled with by the men in our lives, regardless of that male's role.

And ladies, face it, this myth is so enlarged that when God calls us to preach or pastor, if we are married, the first thing we want to do is drag our spouses into the fold, transfer part of our anointing on him. I like the way Tyler Perry's Madea© says it, "Hell, to the No!"

There have been many times when I've heard an anointed, powerful female pastor or teacher say that God is working on my husband John or Bob or Jake and he's going to come on in and be co-pastor or co-whatever. It's as if women have no authority of our own. I've heard many female leaders say their husband is their "covering" or they have to get permission from their (usually male) pastor before they can accept an invitation to preach.

On rare occasions do I hear that men wait around for their wives to be snatched up by the Spirit before they claim their anointing and calling. What's the scripture: "….let us throw off everything that hinders and the sin that so easily entangles. And let us run with perseverance the race marked for us." Jesus came to offer us an alternative way of living. We as women don't seize it. We don't maximize it. We settle. We forget that God favors us—each of us, women, men, children, all of creation. We lose confidence in God's unfailing and unconditional love for us.

We begin to see the men in our lives as the closest we can ever be to God, and oh my, we are encumbered with a sad state of affairs.

It is indeed a misogyny to accept that when the male gender is used, it automatically includes the female. If this is truth, then while you read, when the female gender is used, it is my hope that men will see themselves included in the narrative. Scriptures are written like that. Except, of course, when the male gender needs to exert power, control, and authority over the female, then it's specifically male rather than all inclusive. Another lesson on truth that is not always truth. Misogyny.

I was shocked when I first learned that religion was a human construct in my Sociology-Anthropology course at my undergraduate university. That floored me. Now, over 40 years later, I understand why so much about religion is flawed, even the church's teaching about God. I often wonder how we would know anything about God if not for religion, which is of human origin, and by definition flawed, like many scientific theories that have become defunct over the years. I confess my disappointment in religion, all of them, most specifically, the one that has nurtured me from birth. I confess my dismay that the wonderful truths of the gospel: freedom, liberation, peace, acceptance, inclusion, forgiveness, love--are hidden under a bushel because, it seems, the church is not ready to know the truths that will set us free.

You're probably wondering why there is so much about religion in these pages. I grew up religious. Very. Pentecostal Holiness. Church of Christ Disciples of Christ. Baptist. Freewill Baptist. Mormon. And most everything in between. What can I say? We are what we eat. I've come to realize that much about religion is so "manmade" that it literally sucks. You know what else, I question just about everything there is to question in our sacred text. I even question what makes it sacred. The stories of slaughter, oppression, discrimination, child sacrifice, misogyny of women, roles and place of men and women and children, even the Trinity.

Try as I might, I still can't make three become One and I graduated from a very prestigious Theological Seminary. How does the church explain that God became flesh and became Jesus when the church also says that because we are flesh we are sinners and God can't even see us without the "blood" of "His" son covering us? Oh, and the "he" thing. Please. Go ahead. Brand me. I love God. God loves me. Not the schizophrenic one, as my friend Gwendolyn Blue sometimes say. The One true and living God who created all, gave birth to all, in Her image—that of love and beauty and life. That's the God I know. The Mother of us all. And yes, also the Father of us all. Our Holy Parent.

"But we have this treasure in jars of clay to show that this all-surpassing power is from God and not from us. We are hard pressed on every side, but not crushed; perplexed, but not in despair; persecuted, but not abandoned; struck down, but not destroyed." 2 Corinthians 4:8-9. NIV

INTRODUCTION

There are countless fiction and nonfiction writings by Christian authors. I've appreciated them for their intrinsic value about the Christian's relationship with God and each other. One of the central themes that run throughout these writings is how "nice" everyone speaks. It seems that the writings smooth out the cracks before we even know what the cracks are. And there are so many scriptures to support the evil, vile mistreatment of the heroine or hero. I've lived a different life. I offer no palatable clichés, unquestionable answers, or easily digested placebos for why ish happens. This has caused me to wonder if I'm the only Christian on the planet who has had a different kind of experience. My life has been quite complex. It has been interwoven with a little heaven, and a whole lot of hell. Am I the only person who has lived a life where your man of God has called you a mother fucker just one time too many? Or where the church has turned her back on you, made you feel dirty and inconsequential, because you have given birth to a beautiful son without her sanction.

Am I the only parent who has buried a truly wonderful, loving, respectful son who was seen as invisible in the eyes of the powers that be because he sold drugs and therefore "deserved what he got"? People are never one dimensional. I've learned to look at the world, faith, God, church, others, in 3-D, without the colored lenses that so easily distort my view. Parker Palmer (Circle of Trust©) has taught me to "turn to wonder" as I explore the world and the people around me. Wonder about my reactions and responses, question why I feel the way I do, or think what I'm thinking. Turn to wonder. Amazing the difference this one small nuance can make.

Many times I've pondered the existence of God. I've often asked, "Where is God now? Where was Jesus then? Where even is the church in this?" The answers have disappointed me, often. To all three questions. My experiences have taught me that nothing is black or white; there is an abundance of shaded areas. What I've learned is that there are no easy answers to life's stuff. It is what it is [in the words of my oldest son who was the victim of a senseless murder in Durham, North Carolina]. Yes. Where was God then? Gun violence is a staple in our country. We wouldn't know how to live without it. Many of the "saved, sanctified, and fire baptized" saints would protest legislation against being able to carry a weapon quicker than these same saints would advocate for the rights of women to make decisions about their own bodies, and for the rights of wives and children to be protected from abusive husbands and violent, alcoholic fathers, including institutions, including the church.

Yes. I've witnessed a lot in this life. Two marriages. One ended in divorce. I loved that man. He was my first—in every way. The other, in death. His, of course, Since I'm writing this story. They were both good, decent, men. I'm sure their momma's loved them, had high hopes for them to be bankers or scholars or even president. How would I know? All I know is what they were as husbands and fathers in our relationships.

As you know from the cover page, you are about to meet Melanie, a woman who has been at the bottom, and has won each hurdle, one day at a time. Don't be misled. The drama that is about to unfold before you is not a female story, it encompasses the whole of humanity. The heroine is female, whom society gives permission to cry, hurt, struggle. Men are faced with obstacles and difficulties that society all but forbids men to speak of. They aren't permitted to cry, hurt, scream, lash out, for fear of being perceived as less than men. Men will find themselves caught in the intricate web of Melanie's story. No matter who you are, or where on life's journey you reside, cast yourself in the role of heroine by seeing in Melanie's struggles similarities to your own. If you dare to face the truth. In many ways, most of us have been *cast down*, yet with the innate power of the Creator, we rise from the ashes and move forward to our purpose!

I'm writing this story because the heroine mirrors my own search for truth. Meet Melanie. As a girl struggling to grow up and make sense of a life that never was what it appeared. She grew up in an era when one could not ask questions, of the church, parents, elders; one could only believe and accept because this was God's will, what God needed in order to love us and save us from a burning hell. God required blind trust and obedience to save us and take us to heaven." Hell. Heaven. What a concept. A girl who grew up wanting to be loved and accepted but found this an elusive enigma that was meant for others, never for her.

Within these pages, you will travel with Melanie as sibling rivalry impedes her self confidence, robs her spirit, and foils her attempts to move forward when life is wearing her down. It is a story of growing up too soon, never being the child one was meant to be. This is the story of a teenage mom who became a wife and mother of two very early in life; a woman who loved her husband and desired to please him above all else and make him happy. It's the story of a mature woman, loving a different husband, with two additional children, realizing that life is not a fairytale. It's hard. Harsh. Unforgiving. It's the journey of an older woman who has been through the fires and storms of life only to realize that, despite the teachings of the church to dehumanize her by teaching her that she is dirty, wretched, unclean, "filthy rags" [just writing it here makes me gag], finds that she has had God's favor her entire life.

Melanie's story also is one of triumph, as she rises from the ashes of despair to become a phoenix, that magnificent bird that defies all odds and soars above them with majesty and grace. It is a story of questions about God, faith, eternity, daily bread. That's what life is, you know. As you encounter Melanie within these pages, perhaps you, also, will find her to be a woman after God's own heart. Her story speaks to a faith that discovers God is always with her because She lives inside Melanie, as her conscious and guide. God is her *Inner Teacher*© (Parker Palmer). Or, in the words of Dr. Earl Jerry Griffin, God is her *Inner Conductor*.

My hope in sharing this story is not to alienate the church or my spiritual family. Melanie is a realist. Like Peter (the Apostle), she often speaks what she feels or jumps into unchartered waters with no concern for the raging storm. She knows her life and message will be a stretch for many, but then so was Jesus' life and ministry. Truth in its purest form is known to cut asunder and separate even the closest of friends and family. Melanie offers a word of hope to some girl or boy, woman or man, who has lost hope in God and the witness of the church, and finds him or herself struggling with life questions. As you journey with Melanie, do not expect her to provide answers for life's stuff. It is my hope that you will continue your search for truth and wholeness.

Through all that Melanie lived, losing faith in humanity and herself, she never completely lost her faith in God. That faith brought her a long way. And it will be that faith that will guide her forward. That faith strengthens her in adversity, in uncertainty, doubt, confusion and despair. That faith comforts her and gives her peace. Melanie finds that this faith in God, God's favor, is really her final acceptance that she has all she needs inside herself to be all she wants to be in this life, to live fully imago Dei. Melanie finds that the God she seeks, the favor she seeks, is simply a belief in herself, finding within herself, God.

As you journey with Melanie, open your heart to experience her darkest despair and greatest joys. Her life is filled with twists and turns, ups and downs, sanity and craziness, and some moments when it's almost impossible to imagine what way she will turn. Join her in her triumphs, as she begins to understand that she is the "master of her destiny (fate), the captain of her ship (soul)."

A word of caution. This story is not written for you to judge, criticize, label, or define Melanie's status as a follower of Jesus. You don't get to play God in her life. Ever. Under no circumstances. It is written to speak truth to power in one woman's journey. I can safely tell this story, because despite what you might think, I know that God favors Melanie, and God favors me. As you read, know that I am unencumbered, uninhibited, and uncensored. Like my heroine, I am *living out loud and having my say*. Turn the page. Read at your own peril! Read with an open heart and mind.

The PHOENIX – RISING FROM THE ASHES

INVICTUS, by William Ernest Henley

Out of the night that covers me, Black as the Pit from pole to pole,
I thank whatever gods may be for my unconquerable soul.
In the fell clutch of circumstance I have not winced nor cried aloud.
Under the bludgeonings of chance my head is bloody, but unbowed.
Beyond this place of wrath and tears looms but the Horror of the shade,
And yet the menace of the years finds, and shall find, me unafraid.
It matters not how strait the gate, how charged with punishments the scroll.
I am the master of my fate: I am the captain of my soul.

CHAPTER 1

I'm not surprised that the day began cool and wet. I no longer bothered with weather forecasts. What did they know anyway? After all, my whole life with this man had been more stormy than partly cloudy and sunny. Why would this day be any different? I admit that I was not prepared for the day's ending. I could not have predicted it. There were just enough warm rays from the sun to make our move from a small, rural town in the piedmont area of North Carolina to a small town about 30 minutes east, bearable.

Between intermittent showers and occasional appearances of the sun, we loaded the truck and emptied one house, as we prepared to begin a new chapter in our new home. Tension was high between us. William had waited until the last moment to accept that we had to move from our home. As yet, I'm sure neither of us sensed that our day would become as cold as the frigid -15 degree ice storm that was barreling through Redding, Connecticut at that moment.

We continued our task of packing, loading, cleaning. At ages 16 and 15, our sons were very helpful in this laborious process. On one hand, the move had the potential of being a labor of love; on the other, not so much. It was simply a chore, something we had been forced to do because I decided I would not continue to be the man and the woman, the husband and the wife, the mother and father—dang, the every doggone thing in this marriage of 16 years. I was fed up and I was at a point of no return. As a matter of fact, I was on constant alert, calming myself as best as I could. William had become unpredictable. His mood swings varied and sometimes skyrocketed out of control.

To hell with it! If this man did not take matters into his own hands, find the money we needed to stay in our home then we'd move out. It had come to just that. We were moving. He hadn't even found us a place to live, though he knew that this day was looming on the horizon. I had done that too. Had to. My sons could not live on the streets. As usual, he was content to wait for me to make everything all right.

I lived into his expectations. Found the house in the ninth hour. Made the arrangements with the owner to move in. All William had to do was get someone to help him move our belongings. I'll be doggone. He couldn't even do that right. I think it was in that moment, witnessing the frustration of the move and the nonchalant attitude he showed that I decided I could no longer live with him. I wanted out. The love and trust had diminished years earlier but the commitment I made had held me in bondage. So much had transpired between us…ugly, heartless, downright mean. Looking at him, I knew I could no longer live with him. Had I come to hate this man with whom I once wanted to love and spend the rest of my life?

I finally understood that this chance of new beginnings was pertaining not only to the physical move, but the need for emotional and spiritual re-creation. I knew within my soul that this would be my only opportunity to do something about me, for me, to put myself first for a change. I often tell my students "God has not given you a spirit of fear, but of power and wisdom." It was time that I believed my own teachings. As challenging as it was, in that moment, I spoke up. All fear was gone. Strength welled up from deep within the bowels of my heart and spirit. All my anguish rushed up in this last resolve.

With a degree of calm I did not understand, I began to appeal to my husband. "William, I don't think you and I should move in together this time." I was not prepared for the look of pure hatred and incredulity on his face. "What the hell do you mean by that," he retorted? "We haven't been good together for a long time," I replied, as nervous energy gripped my mind and heart. "I don't know what you're talking about," William said as he advanced towards me. Fear threatened to erode my resolve but I refused to back down. "We should separate for awhile," I stated. "I'm not saying we have to divorce, but we need some time apart, to think about our relationship and plan how we can work on what is causing our problems. I can no longer live with you, William."

I felt the hairs begin to rise on the back of my neck. Not a new sensation. Truth be told, it has happened more often in the past few years than I can count. William literally began to swell right in front of me. Eyes dilated. Pupils almost nonexistent. What was that in his eyes? "There's not a damn thing wrong with our marriage. You are the problem. Always running your mouth. You need to learn how to shut the hell up." Every nerve ending in my body was on high alert. "William, there is something wrong with our marriage. I don't want to keep living with you like this. All I'm asking is that we separate for awhile. Reflect on what we need and want. See a counselor together. But I don't want to do this anymore. I think it's best that you don't come with us right now."

Austin and Aubrey must have sensed something amiss for within a few minutes of our conversation, both sons came to the bedroom where William and I were completing our packing and loading. The looks on their faces were one of uncertainty and yes, fear. I was more convinced than ever that it was time for William and me to go our separate ways, until we could figure out next steps, with the help of a trained marriage counselor.

I picked up my last bag, told our sons to go outside. With another look around, determined to remain calm and not show fear, I began what could have been my last stand, as I moved towards the back door. Wouldn't you know I was all the way at the front of the house which meant I had to remain rational, quiet, and when I did speak, conciliatory so that I could make it through the house and out the back door without causing a scene.

"William," I said, "I'm not asking for a divorce. I'm saying that we have some issues that are bigger than we are. We need help. You have to see the signs. This is not good for us, for the boys." Aubrey and Austin had remained inside, standing just to the right of the back door, near the dryer. "Aubrey. Austin. Take the rest of your bags outside and get in the truck please." After looking at their dad and me, they began to move towards the door. They fidgeted, in no hurry to leave me inside with William. I urged them forward, as I began to move more quickly towards the door. Once they were on the steps, time seemed to stand still. I heard William's stealthy gait behind me, which was a miracle for him, since only a year ago he had recovered from a partial foot amputation. I pushed open the door, and bounded down to my candy apple red 2008 GMC Denali.

It was then that I noticed our sons still hanging around as if unsure whether to get inside or help their dad. "Boys, get in the truck." With one final glance at the menacing look on William's face, they both lunged for one of the doors. "Hurry please," I pleaded, as I ran around to the driver's side and jumped in."Roll up the windows." Once inside, I pressed the door lock switch as William was about to reach for the front passenger door handle. The look in his eyes was even more frightening than any of the other times he had been on the brink of destructive behavior. It could have been because he felt he was fighting for his life, for his family, and for all he knew that was good and wholesome. I will not assume what was going on inside his head. All I know is, that was why I was fighting.

In my frenzy, I started the ignition and pressed the automatic power window button. William continued to pull on the door handles, as he spoke words that shattered my heart and reverberate within my spirit even now. Words that were filled with malice, hurt, anger, frustration, pain, maybe even hate. As I pulled out of the driveway of our old home, to begin a path that would sever a marriage of almost 16 years, William shouted: "Ya'll aint nothing but a bunch of stupid mother-fuckers!"

"Thin line between love and hate" — The Pretenders

It's a thin line between love and hate; it's a thin line between love and hate.
...The sweetest woman in the world could be the meanest woman in the world if
you make her that way
you keep hurting her she'll keep being quiet she might be holding something inside
that'll really, really hurt you one day...you couldn't believe the girl would do
something like this, ha you didn't think the girl had the nerve but here you are
I guess action speaks louder than words
It's a thin line between love and hate

CHAPTER 2

I thought that I should be amazed, astonished even. As I pulled away from the back of the house, directed my smooth Denali down the driveway of our home for the last time, and turned left onto Mabley Drive, an emotion overwhelmed my senses. It was not one of dismay or pain. It was sadness. Deep, uncensored, woe. I was raw. Open. Vulnerable. My thoughts raced through my mind with a frenzy I could not contain. Hot. Vapid. Burning. This man who should have been, in my view, privileged and honored that this woman had looked at him and chose to be his wife, had spoken with such hatred.

Our sons were silent behind me, lost in their own little worlds. I could offer them nothing in that moment. I experienced a powerful urge to pray. Pull over. Stop driving. Breathe. Pray. The Denali had a mind of its own. Flight. Get as far away from this evil presence as possible. Quickly. I continued to drive. Onto 85S, changing directions just long enough to ensure that William was not following us. It was a moment for new beginnings. I continued to drive on unfamiliar streets and scenery from Charlotte to Matthews, where our new residence awaited us, reflecting on the way my life was about to channel unchartered waters and unfamiliar territories.

Less than an hour after I parked in front of the new place, William pulled in. This time, my body recoiled in utter fear. I didn't know what, but had a keen sense something would happen this time, that his presence would escalate into rage and someone would be hurt. I was under the carport; everyone else was inside. He unloaded the remainder of the household furnishings. Then turned to me.

"Where am I supposed to stay if I don't stay here with you all?", he asked. With a serenity I did not know I had, I responded: "I suggest you go back to the country and stay with your mom. It will only be until we can get some things worked out." His nostrils flared like a startled horse sensing an ominous disaster. "I don't know what's wrong with you. I'm staying right here with you and our boys. I'm not going to no damn country." "William," I began, responding with a resoluteness I did not feel. My whole body was tensed in knots, "yes, that's what you will need to do. Or you can call your cousin Leandra and her husband. I'm sure they will let you stay with them for awhile."

I started inside the screened foyer to the kitchen. With a sound akin to rushing water, William grabbed me from the rear, swirling me to face him. 'I'm staying right here. You aren't making any sense. There is nothing wrong with our marriage. I didn't move all this stuff over here today for you to tell me I can't stay here." Mindful that our Austin and Aubrey, Natalia, and Pebbles (daughter and granddaughter) might hear the commotion and come to investigate, I forced my way back to the carport. "William," I began with resignation, "you can't stay here. We have to separate. This is just not working and I no longer want to stay in it."

Call it a final battle cry or a plea of desperation, but in that moment I felt a pressure on my shoulders, along with a powerful force on my arms as William grabbed my 5'3," 120 lb frame and forced me to stand so close to him I could see the hairs inside his nose. But it was his eyes that elicited a primal fear within the core of my being never experienced before. Red. Bulging. Manic. I've heard of these kinds of Jekyll and Hyde transformations. This was my first experience this close. And it was something to behold.

In that instant, I recalled being hospitalized a few months earlier. Blood transfusion. Two pints of blood. A stranger's blood being infused into my body because this man, who promised to love and cherish me, had upset my equilibrium in such a way that my body reacted violently, organs shut down, blood leaving my body through no definable exit site. I had to cancel a trip to Cleveland, Ohio where I served on the Justice and Witness Ministries Board for our national body of the United Church of Christ. Two and a half days in the hospital. He did not visit me. I made an excuse for him. "He had recently had his foot amputated and it was too much for him," I had told my daughter. In the end, no diagnosis. "We don't know what is wrong, Mrs. Bell." Where had I heard those words before?

My mind was made up. I would either die this day or William would walk away until a later time. I was determined that he would not step foot into our new home to live. I don't know what came over me. With a calmness I did not expect, and a fierceness unlike anything I had experienced, I extricated my arm from his grip, stepped up to him and demanded that he leave, just walk away. William was not impressed. He stepped in my space and pressed me against the wall, pinning me with both arms, powerfully exerting his strength and size into my small frame as if daring me to challenge him again, or give him a reason to use his fist against my head.

I knew that feeling. It was not new to me. Once, when our oldest son was barely four weeks old, he had hit me with such force I reeled to our bed. The unexpectedness and force of his iron clad fist connecting with the right side of my jaw stung me in its intensity and hate. His reason? I disrespected him by insisting that I nurse my son after William told me not to do so. One of William's friends was in the car with us.

Of course, he apologized. Went to church. Confessed before everyone. Dragged me to the altar to pray. Forgiveness all around. What a mighty God we serve! Everyone is happy. I never forgot that. Couldn't have if I'd wanted to. The pain in my jaw continued for weeks. Went to D.C. with us on a family vacation and back. I had never experienced this kind of physical abuse or pain before.

Another time, he had obviously had a bad day. I believe the drug use had started by then, though at the time I was unaware of it. William's sister-in-law had come to visit. When she left, William was out of sorts. Who knows what set him off? The slightest little thing could at any given moment. I remember saying something about him not eating dinner I think. He mumbled in response about dinner not being fit for anyone to eat. Of course, I suggested that he could fix his own food. And *whack*, a smack to my head. Again.

There was the time we were at a church service one night. Our choir had to sing. Before the worship service began, William made a statement about what we were singing that night. I countered with a nonchalant remark about the fairness our musician used in choosing leaders for the songs. William told me I just needed to keep my mouth "shot" [his vernacular for shut] and leave that kind of thing to the musician. And I said, I'm leaving it to the musician but I had a right to speak if I had something to say. In the next instance, I felt a hand go around my neck and a harsh voice say to me, "I said keep your mouth "shot!" That very moment, one of William's cousins walked by. "What's up cuz?" he asked. William removed his hand from around my neck. "Ain't nothing," he responded, smiling up at Maxton.

I knew from experience what fear and violence does to a woman when it's enacted on her by the man who is supposed to love and cherish her. From the time I was old enough to understand, I had witnessed my Dad beating my mother. I heard her wimp and plead with him, and he hit her until he was satisfied. At least, that's as I remember it. This was no different. I used to think that if my Mother had just kept her mouth "shot" my Dad would stop hitting her. I knew better now. I also knew that she could not keep quiet. She had to try to talk some sense into the man she loved, even when it seemed only to exacerbate the situation.

I had learned to live on pins and needles in William's presence or at the thought that he would soon be present. I had learned to walk on egg shells in every way, to keep my mouth "shot." Maybe my mother had also. That would explain why she wanted us to be particularly quiet when "Ben " [we called our Dad by his first name] was around. I had taught our sons that also. "Just don't say anything to antagonize your Dad sons," I would caution. The oldest son, Aubrey, was good at this. He found other, more subtle ways to show his displeasure. He would move slower than the situation dictated. Take longer to do what his Dad asked him to do. Austin could be quite defiant! The younger one—where did he get such lip?

Yes, that's how far we had regressed. I was no longer an adult in my own home. Except in the ways I found to be passive aggressive. A new character trait. One I never learned to be proud of, but felt my life depended on it. Quite frankly, even the life and peace of my sons' lives. I became really adept at living in this way. Didn't say a lot. Found ways to make known my displeasure. Not this time. Standing under the carport I knew I could no longer keep my mouth shut. I would speak, even if it cost my life. My resolve to live free, to come out of bondage in a relationship that had simply sucked the life right out of me was overwhelming. I could no longer control the instinctive primal response to flight or fight. I could not run, not any more.

As we stood under the carport, William became consistently more irate and belligerent in his tone and manner. My cajoling had no effect on him. He was beginning to wear me down. I felt my resolve weakening. He would not let up. As I moved further inside the carport, away from the kitchen door, everything within me screamed to hold my ground. How could I? This was my husband. The father of our two sons. He had been there to help support my oldest children. He gave my daughter, Natalia, her first car, and taught my oldest son, Malek, how to fish. In spite of the fact that my oldest son had shot William in both legs, which almost left him handicapped, this man had been there for me and my children in many ways, even when their own father had abandoned them.

"William," Malek asked. "Where those fishing poles at? Time to drop them in the water, ain't it?"

"We can hit it right now. You ready?" A broad grin spread across my husband's face.

"Poles right here in the trunk. You got some worms?" Malek was happy to go with his step father to the lake.

"Nothing to it but to do it. Worms ain't no problem. Let's git to gittin it!"

And off they went. "Frying pan," I heard William say with a broad grin from ear to ear. They'd stay for hours, until dusk most times. When they returned, always with a meal of course, William and Malek would clean fish, cook them, and we'd have a feast of hush puppies, slaw, and fish. Talking about some good eating, great laughs. This was family time the way it was designed to be. I was always grateful that our family times did not end up like my mother's when I was little. William and I did not spend all our time fighting or fussing. Actually, I wasn't much good at that, anyway. I'd clamor up at the first hint of conflict.

In those memorable moments, William was the Father who had been a father when the real father was not. He would stop whatever he was doing when this son came around. Not just to fish. Work on a car. Go see a man about a mule. There was no limit to what these two did together. It was doing these idyllic interruptions in our normal lives that I heard William say for the first time: "one man's junk is another man's treasure." He was referring to my divorce from my first husband. After dismantling the negative pun of "junk," I decided that he had a great point.

There were the times we would have cookouts. Both my husband and son could cook. They spent many wonderful evenings on the patio cooking, bragging about whose deep fried turkey was the best, or who had burned the hole into the back deck.

When Malek shot William, a hatred developed deep within his heart towards this son. My son did not shoot out of malice; he shot to protect his sister. That little girl was his heart. He lived by the sword; ultimately, he died by it. It took a lot of prayer and tender loving care on my part to restore that relationship. A relationship that William's family fought against; they did not want the two to reconcile. Family. Sometimes, family should butt out of immediate family's stuff. Let them work out their lives together.

Often, William would come home, weary, burdened, because his sisters (two in particular) called him a fool for reconciling with our son. "I want Penelope and Janice to stay out of my face with that mess. This is our family. They don't live over here. Malek and I are alright. I've forgiven him. He has forgiven me. We've moved on." I would hold him those times. I, too, was pleased that their relationship was on the mend. It would never be what it was, of course. How could it be? They were living at peace with each other.

I admit my son could not understand why I stayed in the relationship. "Ma, I gave you an out, and you still stayed with that crazy man. I don't want to hear any more complaints from you about him." There was nothing for me to say. My explanations rang hollow even in my own ears. "I am William's wife, son. He needs me here." Would it make any logical sense to anyone that I felt God wanted me to stay with that man? I can't explain it. I just knew I had to stay. William's recuperation took almost a year. Several surgeries, bed pans, checkups, metal leg brace, wheelchair, disrespect, rudeness, anger, bitterness. That was my life and William's, and yes, our children. He soon became strong again. In every way. And yes, there were times when I questioned my own decision to stay. There was one time I remember distinctly.

I had begun working part time in order to take care of him. The doctors at the prestigious hospital where I served as Administrative Supervisor, had begun to financially contribute to our monthly income, not only because of my work with them. William was a favorite of my staff. One of the doctors was our family doctor. This staff gave me all the time off I needed to care for my husband. One particular day I came home. Tired. If you've ever provided care for a person who is bedridden and dependent on you for everything, you know what I mean. My mother-in-law had been my strongest support during this time. She was there when I arrived, leaving a few minutes later.

William asked me to bring him the bed pan. I had noticed that each time I arrived home, it seemed that his internal bowels clock would time the hour for his waste release. This particular day, I just couldn't deal with that. "William," exasperation seething through every word, "if you had to get on the pot, why did you wait until I walked through the door?" I asked. "Bring me the damn bed pan before I shit on this bed," he responded. By reflex, I reached for the bedpan. Something made me stop. Was that venom I heard in his voice? "I tell you what," I responded with a sound akin to hatred in my voice. "If you don't get up out of this bed and go the bathroom, you will certainly mess up your clothes. I'm tired of you and your shit!" With that, I walked out of the room.

Mind you, I chose to stay and take care of this man. People were calling me a fool, saying I was stupid for staying with him, putting up with his crap. Those who knew me best were surprised that I had dated or married him. And now he's just going to make demands out of pure spite! Needless to say, I heard him pulling on the rails over the bed. I heard the wheel chair being pulled to the bed. That man got up, went to the bathroom, and from that day throughout his recovery, not once did I have to empty his bedpan again. William was not one who welcomed being dependent on anyone. In addition, I found out that day that he had already started taking steps from time to time. No one told me. Not even him. He applauded me for taking a stand. Was resentment beginning to grow within me?

No. All of our time together had not been horrible. There were many days when we laughed. Nights when we loved. Months when we struggled and talked and planned for our future together. I had already divorced once. What kind of woman would I be if I divorced again? How could God possibly love me and continue to call me beloved and highly favored if I, once again, renounced my marital covenant and put this father and husband into the streets? On top of that, what kind of witness could I possibly offer other women or even the church as I preached and ministered in song and word? Who would want to hear from a woman like me? Guilt was about to overpower me as I waged the battle to give in or stand my ground. I could not abide conflict. My stomach was all in knots. Fear was closing in once again.

The beauty of the soul shines out when a man bears with composure one heavy mischance after another, not because he does not feel them, but because he is a man of high and heroic temper. – Aristotle

CHAPTER

3

Whether providence, happenstance, or just what, I will never know. As my resolve was weakening and William was becoming progressively loud, the kitchen door opened. Natalia, my daughter, had heard the commotion and came to investigate. She took one look at me, another at William, and summed up what for her was just about enough. She threatened William, told him to leave, and said he would not be coming into that house. The thing is, there was never any love lost between these two and this day would prove to be the last straw for both of them.

Natalia did not mince words. She had been an outspoken child from the time she was just a wee little girl, demanding her right to be heard and obeyed, actually. Amazing how a child can have such a commanding presence that follows her throughout life. There were times in school when teachers would call me because Natalia dared speak against some of their decisions regarding her, in particular disciplinary measures. I was often so proud of her for having the courage to be in ways that I've secretly coveted. Neither her mother nor grandmother possessed that kind of boldness.

Natalia stepped up to William, told him to leave. The argument that ensued between them was awful. Needless to say, everything they had held within themselves at my expense erupted, like hot salty ash from an overflowing volcano. Words. Actions. Both said what had languished in their hearts and minds for 16 years. Their words and actions stirred a primal reflex within me that had lain dormant for too long. It is safe to say here that I could always face William with less fear when Natalia was within close proximity.

William stepped one time too many into this woman's space. Next thing I knew, she had grabbed a shovel; William snatched up a rake and they were at each other. I believe Natalia was the first to swing. Then all hell broke loose. Hateful words. Anger. Bitterness. My daughter and my husband were fighting like the Jerry Springer kind of uncensored battling. No holes barred. It was all I needed. People say they will never do this or that. They say real Christians won't fight, cuss, kick, scream, kill. I don't know about that. What I do know is, when I saw this man, whom I had lain with, cooked for, cleaned while he was sick, laughed with, fought with, praised God with, this man I had called "husband" for 16 years, pick up a rake and walk up to my daughter in a menacing way, all of my initial determination to get away from him arose within my bowels.

Something else too, a different emotion. An emotion I had worked hard to keep out of my thoughts and heart—hate. In that moment, a raw primitive hatred overtook me and in my insanity, I picked up a hoe [who left these weapons of mass destruction so handy when they moved away?] and began to strike William, everywhere. I didn't care where. I gave no consideration to what would happen next. My senses were on high alert; my actions were instinctive—protect my daughter and yes, my own life.

I did not "lose my religion." I put on the whole armor of God to stand against the "wiles" of the damned devil. That's what I did. And that's what Natalia did also. Yolanda Adams sings a song that says "the battle is not yours, it's the Lord's". Maybe. But under that carport, neither of us was concerned about that. Each of us, it seems, was fighting for what we believed was right. Do I condone violence? No. Will I fight? Provocation begs a response.

To his credit, William fought a gallant fight. He was physically not well. He fell under the assault. I recall William looking up at me, from the floor where he was now cowed, defending himself against the blows from the shovel Natalia was swinging and the hoe I held in my hand. With a sound akin to utter disbelief and perhaps even respect, he said, 'I can't believe you would hit me like this.' By this time, our youngest son, Aubrey, had walked outside. I told him to call the police. He looked at me as if to say, "what do you mean; that's daddy." "Aubrey, call the police," I instructed. He could tell by the tone of my voice that this was a serious matter, and he did as I asked him. "You too Aubrey," said William. "You calling the police on your daddy, boy"?

I ached for Aubrey. What kind of psychological damage were we inflicting on this innocent young man child, of only 15 years? But the police had to be called. William would not give up. And I knew that someone would be seriously hurt if law enforcement did not intervene. I wanted William out of my life; in that instant, I was willing to do everything I could to make sure he was out, and stayed out. Never had I felt such hatred towards another human being as in the moment when that man picked up that rake and attacked my child. I wonder if Natalia ever realized what it took for me to stand up to him that day. To grab the shovel and come to her defense in a way I had not done prior to this. I didn't even do anything when he snatched the necklace from around her neck and broke it. Our youngest son, Aubrey, relayed something very sobering to me once.

"Mom," he said, "my childhood was horrible. I never liked it after we moved to Charlotte. I always had a terrible feeling that something bad would happen and you would not be there to stop it." I looked at him, as we drove down 85S on our way to the mountains of North Carolina. "What do you mean, Aubrey? Why didn't you tell me you felt like that? I thought I had done a good job protecting you and Austin from seeing the ugliness in our family." My heart was about to explode once again. "No ma'am," he said. "You weren't the one daddy was saying all those bad things to. You didn't get a crutch thrown at you. Austin never got treated like that either. It was just me."

We spoke about how Austin was the favored child, of his dad and his dad's family, and how Aubrey always felt like an outsider, an outcast to be exact. "Even today when I visited my in-laws, Mom," Aubrey continued. "The first words were not 'how are you, it's good to see you'. The words were, 'when have you heard from Austin'." With a heavy sigh, I apologized to this son. "That's why I was happy when Natalia moved in with us, and when she came back from California," Aubrey continued. "I knew that she would keep bad things from happening." I often wonder if Natalia has ever forgiven me for my weakness in those days. Now, I have to find a way to rectify what I had permitted to happen to this child also. With further conversation, I'm sure to find out what Austin has been holding in all these years. Healing comes with confession and forgiveness. We cannot change what was, but we can begin anew.

This man had me so timid I sometimes blamed my 13 year old daughter for his rudeness and inexcusable behavior. "If you would just stop talking so much and do what he asks you to do, Natalia," I would say to her. 'You really do have way too much mouth." Those scenes came rushing back to me. Once, when I was in Cleveland, William called me about a problem he was having with Natalia. "You had better get her on the phone and tell her to get out of my damn face." He spoke with such venom. What could I do so far away? "William, I am too far away to do anything about that. Just don't say anything to her and I will talk with her when I get back." "I'm sick and tired of that child's mouth," he responded, anger and yes, hurt, in his voice. "She needs to learn to stay out of my face." "I'll call her on her phone and make sure she doesn't come back downstairs to say anything to you," I concurred.

I would call her. She would give me another side of the story, of course. What could I do? How much longer could I be the go between for my daughter and her step father? Why could they not see what their bitterness towards each other was doing to me? It wasn't just my marriage with William that put me in the hospital, it was all of this stuff. All of it. I could never admit that to anyone. What would my daughter think? What would my siblings thing? "You need to get that grown girl out of your house." I had already heard that a couple of times. From siblings. From friends. I would not put her out. She and Pebbles would always have a home with me. Always. William insisted on inviting her back to live with us. Her, her man, and my little girl. No. I would never put them out.

As I looked at the man who had been my husband, those thoughts and more rushed up to me. Whether my daughter was right or wrong, she was my daughter. He had no right whatsoever to raise his fist or any weapon towards her in anger. I would not allow it to happen. Not again. I no longer needed an excuse. When I started hitting him, I have to admit that it felt so liberating, so damn good. All of the pent up emotions and feelings and anguish that I had harbored for so long rose to the surface. I literally felt like shouting halleluia! And that's my good word! Oh, I just wanted him gone. Gone. And in that moment, for a brief second, I wanted to make sure he would be gone forever! I thank God, even today, that we didn't need to hit him often or with undue force. He was a sick man, and could only exert minimum effort.

It seemed to take the officers forever to reach us. Actually, it did take an unreasonably long time (for which they apologized when they finally arrived). In the meantime, both my daughter and I kept William away from the door. I pleaded with him to get in his truck and leave. It wasn't until he heard the sirens that he made any move to leave. I remember him looking at me. He seemed so forlorn. There were a few drops of blood running down his forehead. He turned to me, so pitiful, not so big and bad now. Sad, really. All the fight was gone. "Mark my words," he said, "you will never be anything because of the way you treated me. You just wait and see. You won't ever have anything." Sixteen years. Summed up in a curse. Not just on my life. Our sons. Maybe even down through the generations. If I never amounted to anything, how could our children? I felt bereft. Alone. Afraid. And yes, as strange as it might seem, hopeful.

With those words, and the piercing sounds of the wailing sirens growing distinctively closer, I watched William get into his truck, close the door, and speed off, with all the anger, hurt, amazement, and despair evident in one move. We had married with the intention of loving each other, raising any children we had, and doing big things together. Look at us. It is said that there is a thin line between love and hate. I discovered the truth in those words for myself that day. And, so help me God, so did William.

Let me not pray to be sheltered from dangers, but to be fearless in facing them. Let me not beg for the stilling of my pain, but for the heart to conquer it. Let me not crave in anxious fear to be saved, but hope for the patience to win my freedom. Grant that I may not be a coward, feeling your mercy in my success alone, but let me find the grasp of your hand in my failure. — Rabindranath Tagore

CHAPTER 4

Who would have thought our marriage would have come to this! Just sixteen short years earlier, William and I didn't even know each other. We met at a bake sale and car wash his church was holding as a fundraiser. Can't even recall the reason for the fundraiser now. William was frying fish. He was working so hard. Very diligent. He made some off side comment about how I looked in my shorts. He wasn't disrespectful. As a matter of fact, I found the comment flattering. Never expected anything to come of it. I was there only because my best girl friend was a part of the activity. She had invited me to stop by and buy a dinner.

William was medium height, average build, with a tendency towards chubby. Curly hair. Pecan tan complexion. Mustache. Pleasant personality. People around him seemed genuinely fond of him. We said a few words to each other. He knew what to do with grease, fish, and hush puppies, let me tell you.

Shortly thereafter, my girlfriend, Madeleine, invited me to join a choir she had started at her home church, Rock of the Pines United Church of Christ. I didn't know it at the time, but this was to prove to be a life-changing introduction for me, in more ways than one. Madeleine and I had been friends it seemed for ages, though it had only been about eight years. We met at another church in the Queen City,

Charlotte, where she was very involved in the youth ministries there. About 15 years my junior, we instantly bonded. My children, Malek and Natalia, became her instant siblings, or nephew and niece. The bond was mutual and binding, continuing to this very day. I had left Bentwood Baptist church where we met, but our relationship thrived. Madeline was involved in my life and that of my children in every way. I can see her now. Tall. Willowy. The longest legs ever it seemed! Honey nut complexion. Long, thick mane of dark hair. Beautiful brown eyes. She was a very attractive young lady (girl). With the personality to match. Instant connection between us. My children adored her!

Sometime after I had left Bentwood, I became a Mormon. That's another whole book. Let me say this. I decided I would not subject my beautiful brown children to a doctrine that tells them white is right and anything less is a fright. No offense to any wonderful Mormon sisters and brothers. That was my experience as a member of the Church of Jesus Christ of Latter Day Saints. In addition, I learned that the only way I could get to heaven was to be married to one of the brethren in good standing. Hell. At that time, with only two other brown brothers in the whole place, well, what were my chances? Go figure. A short lived experience in some ways; about two years actually. I had begun to miss church. I think that's why I became a Mormon. I needed that connection with sisters and brothers of the faith. There were some great times. I particularly commend the strong emphasis the Latter Day Saints placed on family and on helping each other in need. I never felt close to anyone. Needless to say, my departure came early.

Several years lapsed between my time as a Mormon and the beginning of my experience at Rock of the Pines United Church of Christ. It was during this interval Madeleine invited me to join her new choir.

"Hey," came this delightful voice across the miles. "It's me!"

"Hello yourself," I responded, as always glad to hear from Madeleine. "I'm calling because I have great news," she said. "Oh Lord," I said with laughter in my heart, thinking she had met another wonderful guy. Madeleine's news was usually filled with tidbits of another 'really nice guy'. I awaited her response with anticipation. 'I've started a choir," she burst out! "A what"? "Where"? Immediately, my ears and eyes were wide open to this news! "At my church, Rock of the Pines United Church of Christ. I need you to join. I know how much you love to sing. You would love the people. They're a good group!"

Madeleine raced on with more about this choir and her excitement was completely contagious. I had so missed singing and being with a faith community. By this point, I was ready to give the institutional church another chance to embrace me as a daughter of God. "I'll do it," I said. "When is rehearsal?" After filling me in on the details, I agreed to meet her on the scheduled date and time and attend my first choir rehearsal. As she stated, it was a good group. Except this one guy who was a bit unorthodox. He was the comedian of the group. A member of the family who had started that church and so was tolerated well by most members, even Madeleine.

I remember the first night of rehearsal. One of the female members said something to me to indicate that she would fight if she had to. It came out of nowhere. And I retorted that I could fight too and no one was afraid of her. The guy who was the funny man of the group, took me under his wings right then and there, and told the lady to mind her business and leave me alone, saying I was new and he was certain I had meant no harm by the remark I had made (whatever it was). I do not recall the specific remark. I do know that the lady and I had several of those episodic moments for a while. And the funny guy always had my back. His name was William.

One day the choir, Spirit of Praise, along with our Pastor, Reverend James Dunham, had worshipped with another church in western North Carolina. William and I were walking towards our individual cars and we passed by his mother. William turned to his mother. "Mom, this is going to be your next daughter-in-law," he stated, smiling from ear to ear. "Alright boy," his mother said, looking at me with a large smile. I simply shook my head. William and I had not gone out on a date as of that time. Who knows where that was coming from?

When I asked him about going out with me, he said something about having to tie up some loose ends before he and I could go out. "Be patient," he said. I found this comical. I had not seriously considered going on a date with William. I thought he was someone to play with. Pick on if you will. Not someone to date. This is the same guy who asked our choir director, Madeleine, if we could sing this song one Sunday during worship: "Devil, you can't fool me, I see you behind that tree. Devil, you can't fool me, trying to get your hooks in me!" How do you take someone like that seriously?

Talking with William became a game for me. At first. My intent was to see just how well I could get over on him. Nothing would have come of the game, I don't think. Except, the brother could dance. He was just tall enough to be taller than I was, but not so tall that we couldn't 'fit', you know. One night he had come to see me at my house. I don't exactly recall where Malek and Natalia were, maybe in the bed. William and I started dancing to one of the late great R&B sounds. The brother was smooth. By the time he left that night, I was flat out hot. Point blank. I knew right then he'd have to come back. Me and my libido. Goodness. I never expected to be carrying his child one year later, and subsequently Mrs. William J. Bell, six weeks after that. Here we are, 16 years and two sons later. Look at the mess we got ourselves into.

The seasons teach us two lessons that both steady and chastise: all things must pass, and all things shall return. They tell us that every new beginning brings us closer to an end, and every elegy has within it the echo (and the promise) of a future celebration. They say that love seems eternal now and may soon be a distant memory; and that a new love may come along to revive our sense of eternity. They teach us that suffering is inevitable, and in that inevitability is a constancy that helps take the edge off suffering. Seasons instruct us, then, in a subtler way of being... — Pico Iyer,

Chapter 5

William had spent two nights in jail that fateful weekend. He also was ordered by the courts not to be in contact with me. I didn't know that, of course. My initial attempts at contact had failed. One of those times he answered the phone and informed me of the court's decision. It was during this time that I learned also of a petition that was circulating on his behalf, to speak to his character and integrity. I was being maligned, black balled by friends and family. Branded. The black widow. Remember what I said about labels earlier?

Against my daughter's wishes and appreciation, I called the District Attorney and set up an appointment to speak with her. I wanted to ask for leniency on my husband's behalf. Sometimes, one has to do the right thing even when others don't understand. In spite of everything, I did not feel that justice would be served by locking William away for any length of time, because of his attack. William was not well. Diabetic. Amputee. Heart problems. Possible kidney complications. And of course we didn't know it at that time, but his liver was being invaded by cancerous cells. He had been rendered completely harmless by all of this. Ultimately, I did not want my sons' father to go to prison. The DA granted my request. William was given a year's probation, which was also lifted once I signed a form asking the DA to give him visitation privileges to see his sons, and vice versa.

I was totally unprepared for my daughter's response to my action. "You're going to do what Mother?" Natalia asked. "This crack head almost gave me lockjaw because I was defending you and this household… and.you're gonna go and tell the D.A. that he doesn't deserve to be in jail???!!!" Natalia was completely baffled. She looked at me as if I was some alien life form. Natalia could not believe what I was telling her. She was literally stuck in a 'What da hell?' state of being.

I started to explain that William was sick and that he was no longer a threat to our family. I wanted to convince Natalia that I was doing what I felt was in the best interest for her and her brothers, Alex and Austin. I could not bear the thought of William being sick and being in jail because he wouldn't get the care he needed. My words fell on deaf ears. Blah…Blah…Blah. All that I said…..regardless of what it was… got me nowhere. Natalia had completely tuned me out.

She told me later, she kept saying to herself, "But what about me? What about what I want? Don't you care about what I want? I'm your daughter!!" In her words, she was disappointed…but not. Hurt… but not. Unexpected ….but…..not. She felt that she was used to being put on the back burner when it came to the men in my life. In her view, I continued to 'justify' why my appointment with the DA made the most sense, as she continued to eat applesauce and mashed hot dogs because her jaw popped and ached every time she attempted to move it. She thought to herself, 'Damn, I can't wait for my next therapy session!'"

There was one thing my daughter said she felt that evening. "I gotta admit something though. It was worth it. Finally being able to kick his butt….without fear of my mother's backlash….yeah, the pain in my jaw was well worth it! This man infiltrated our family over 16-17 years ago and managed to lock you into some twilight zone version of a marriage. I remember looking at him once and wondering, 'What da hell does she see in him? Huge smile showing all them damn teeth while saying 'yessuh' to anyone that he thought was better than him. (And trust me; he did it all the time!!)."

As Natalia continued to talk, the hour stretched and stretched, or so it seemed. "Those character voices that you loved to hear him do, annoyed me to death!! I could see him. You couldn't. You were blinded by ….whatever… But I wasn't. I wasn't the one sleeping with that dude and he wasn't my damn daddy so I saw him for what he was worth. Nothing. Absolutely useless. The fact that I dated and married the guy that sold crack to him and his crack head friends didn't help my view of him either. I hated him. His very existence made me wanna slit my own wrists….repeatedly!! So it never made any sense to me that you…. Mother… the apple of my eye and the person who made the sun rise and fall, fell for THIS man!!"

I listened with tears in my eyes. My heart swelled with a feeling close to what one would experience when having an anxiety attack. "You had the skin and beauty of a goddess," Natalia continued. "You had natural beauty. You didn't have to apply anything to 'put your face on' other than Oil of Olay!! (Remember how you always said you were NOT going to grow old gracefully…you were gonna fight it EVERY STEP OF THE WAY!!) At only 5' nothing, you didn't even have to go to the gym and work out. Everything always fit perfectly!! You would put on business clothes or Sunday suits and be the bomb!! You owned the space you walked and moved around in."

What was the look on my daughter's face as she continued in a haunting voice: "And OH MY GOODNESS! SMART??! Yes, I'd fall just shy of calling you a genius. Yeah…BRILLIANT is a good word for you, Mother. Every since I could remember, being intelligent was important. It was a necessity and it was in some ways, the one skill that would take you the farthest in life. You had like four or five degrees and kept going back for more. Hell, being smart was so serious in our house that 'Scrabble' became the favorite past time. If there were a couple of hours that we needed to fill – we broke out the scrabble board!! (P.S. William never played scrabble!) You taught me how to be the bold, courageous, independent and outspoken woman that I am today so you have to understand why you talking to the DA knocked me flat!!"

With resignation, Natalia concluded. "The night you told me about going to the D.A., I put Pebbles to bed around 9pm and replayed the conversation I had with you earlier that day. I was just about to let a tear drop when my phone rang. "Hello?"

"Hey Natalia. You busy baby?"

"I'm putting Pebbles in the bed, David. What's going on witcha?"

"I was hoping to be able to see you tonight. I got about $300 that I don't know what to do with and thought you could come over and help me figure it out." David was one of my best clients. If he said he had $300, I knew I could walk out after about 3 hours with at least $425. I told David to gimme about 45 minutes and I'd be right over. David was the paying diversion I needed, Momma, just what I needed."

I replay that conversation with Natalia over and over in my mind. Tears flow. Gulps. Pain. Distress. A friend had told me that dads do a job on their daughters even when they don't hit. I have come to realize that moms do also. What a lesson. "Train up a child the way she should go and when she is old she will not depart." Proverbs 22:6. I felt my heart drop within my chest. I wondered if I'd ever be able to catch it before it hit rock bottom.

William and I reconciled and reestablished our friendship ten months after the carport incident. When he was diagnosed with liver cancer a year later, though we didn't live together, I was at his side almost every day, from his diagnosis in December until his death three months later. Another great thing is Aubrey and his dad were at peace with each other. This was a very special moment because Aubrey was firmly accepting of his sexuality. William had suspected that this son was different. He never stated in what way he felt this was so.

As an African American male and father, and yes, a Christian, William had a hard time with this. There were many incidences when dad would try to "make" Aubrey be tough, macho, manly. In William's view, Aubrey was too soft. Needless to say, a huge rift developed between them over the years. William's inability or refusal to accept this son was one of the reasons William latched out at Aubrey the day he threw the crutch. That is my belief. I'm certain it's true. During one of the visits to the hospital after William was diagnosed with cancer, William and Aubrey had a chance to speak privately. Father and son were in right relationship again. All was forgiven. What a joy!

"The most beautiful people I've known are those who have known trials, have known struggles, have known loss, and have found their way out of the depths." — Elisabeth Kübler-Ross

CHAPTER

6

William was a good patient. He held onto his faith that God would heal him of the cancer until the moment he died. "If there is any sick among you, let them call for the elders of the church. They will anoint that one with oil, pray the prayer of faith, and the sick will recover." Some would say that God did heal him, that his healing came through death. Whatever. I really need more enlightenment here. These Bible verses sometimes just do not make a lot of sense. Who wrote this stuff! Covered in oil. Prayers from all parts of the County and very far away. Maybe we didn't have the faith "the size of a grain of mustard seed." William died. Very peacefully. I was with him. I held him. I listened to his last breath. His death was one of the most spiritual moments I've shared with him, and there were many. It was mine to share, mine alone. I will always remember him with love and deep fondness, for giving me that gift.

My husband left this world, his sons, mother, me and the other family the way he had entered it. Alone. I was honored to be in the room with him because for two years I had not been welcomed by my husband's family. I had been at my mother-in-law's home one morning when the Hospice nurse came to take care of William. Three of my sisters-in-law were there, along with William's daughter by a much earlier marriage, almost 30 years before we met. As the nurse was speaking and I asked a question, William's family looked at me as if I was the disease, rather than the cancer that was destroying the cells of the one we loved in the next room.

With a rage that had been building inside of me for almost two years, I spoke my truth in that circle. "This is my husband lying in that bed," I began. I felt the tears welling up within me, but was determined to keep them in as I spoke my heart in that room. "You all are treating me as if I have no right to be here. I am the one William married. I am the one who has been with him through all his sickness, partial amputation. I'm the one, along with my mother-in-law, who emptied his bed pan when he couldn't get out of bed on his own. I'm the one who gave him two sons, and have helped him raise those sons. Yes, we have had our difficulties and yes, we had to separate. You don't know what happened under that carport. And you've never asked me. You just sit here acting all important, as if we don't have a history together. We do. He is my husband. William loved me. I loved him as well as I knew how. It is unfortunate that we had our differences. That's over. I'm going to take care of him as best as I can when I can. Get used to it. I'm not going anywhere. I am his health care power of attorney; you need to remember it. We don't have to be great friends. But that is my husband lying back there. Not yours. You will not keep me from doing what I can for him."

I have no idea why I was fighting this hard to be where I was neither wanted, nor needed. There was even a time when the man lying in the back room turned against me. I recalled it vividly. It was late one night. William had turned to me for sexual relations. That is how I had begun to coin our marital bed escapades—just sex. Not because sex was no longer good between us. Because of the many things that had transpired over the years. The love seemed to be missing. This night, William didn't have any condoms. He knew it was a no-no to request sex without one. I was relentless in this one regard only. Tonight would be no different. After attempting to kick me off our bed, William got up, dressed, and headed for the door. He had said some very unpleasant words while dressing; I made no response. But when he started for the door, I asked him not to leave, even grabbing him around his legs to demonstrate my plea. William shook me from his leg, stepped over me, and walked out of our kitchen door, and in my way of thinking, out of our marriage forever. Oh yes, he returned that night. Nothing was ever the same again. Nothing. So. Why was it important to me that I help him through this valley of the shadow of death? I wish I knew the answer. It was not because I was madly in love with him. There was something else. One day, I'll spend time unpacking this emotion. In that moment, I knew that I would take care of my husband. I would not let anyone stop me. I fought my in laws for that right.

It all came rushing out of me. I didn't stop until I said everything I needed to say. When I stopped, the room became very quiet. I turned to the nurse and said, please tell me what I need to do for my husband. Though she had not been guilty of keeping me from the information, she was very cautious, as if she had not been told of the reason for my presence nor the relationship between William and me. From that day until William died, that nurse and all the others who came to care for my husband, treated me with respect, care, and concern. For a couple of years after his demise, I continued to hear from them.

Not so with all but one of my sisters-in-law. They did not treat me bad; I felt tolerated. There continued to be an underlying current of hostility, overall. One of my sisters-in-law, Serena, reached out to me through all of this. Serena was the person I called to the room when William died. Not only was she a nurse, she also was treated as the outsider in her family, which I believe, made her have compassion on me. To the contrary, neither of my brothers-in-law nor my mother-in-law shared the kind of animosity towards me I received from the other sisters-in-law.

William died two years almost to the day we separated, after our fight under the carport of my new residence. In those two years, we reconciled our differences, made confessions, asked for forgiveness. He and I went out a few times. Shopping. Dinner. Most of the time Austin and Aubrey were with us. One of the most memorable occasions was when William joined us at the local high school during Austin's senior year. Austin was being honored as a senior and football player. William and I walked onto the football field together. It was a good moment.

William also attended Austin's graduation. He was a proud father. I was happy for him that day. This was a true accomplishment for him, that one of his boys had graduated high school, after being without children and a family of his own for so very long.

Still, throughout William's sickness and funeral, I had to make my presence known. Once or twice, I was asked my opinion about something. Mostly. Not. I remember William's daughter from a previous marriage, coming to me at the funeral home with sadness in her eyes. "I'm sorry my aunts are treating you like this, Melanie. I know you loved my dad, and I know he loved you." The day of his funeral, my sons and I were made to sit in the second family car while my husband's first wife of about two years over 30 years earlier and their daughter along with his sisters sat in the first family car.

His own mother was left out of that first car. I had to bite my tongue, hard, until I tasted blood in my mouth. My brother, Jeremiah, was my strong tower during this time. His was a calming presence. His words encouraged me, reminding me of who I was (a daughter of God) and my witness to my sons, daughter, family, the world. Jeremiah stayed close by my side. He felt my pain, understood my anguish, and walked me through my angst. Others were there for me also, one of William's cousins, Heaven, and my sister's husband, Sylvester.

The voice of reason and sanity that I remember most is Jeremiah's. The arm around me, the hand that held me, the presence that reminded me of the unconditional love of God, was Jeremiah's. To him I am eternally grateful. Several times I came close to lashing out: at the family house, at the church when we were lining up, and most vehemently at the cemetery. Jeremiah's presence was a soothing influence, the way I imagine God's rod and staff to be. William's aunts, first cousins, church members, our pastor from Rock of the Pines, handled me with a 10 ft pole, or "kid's glove" some would say. There were very few words of comfort for me [or William's sons].

At William's funeral, I celebrated his home going with a song I knew he would understand in ways no one else would: "Wind Beneath My Wings." He had lived in the shadows of my affluence. In many ways, it was because of him I had been able to soar, for both of us. My only regret is that he couldn't be content with my soaring; he had to find a way to clip my wings. Walking from the pulpit area, with my head held high, proud of the wife and mother I had been, I approached my husband's bier, kissed my palm, placed it on the casket, and said goodbye. We had not been perfect together, far from it. We had done our best. Now it was time for him to rest from the troubles and trials of life. It was time for me to move forward. "Thank you William", I said. "I will love your sons and take care of them to the best of my ability." With that, I walked back to my seat with a strong determination and resolve, as the celebration continued. Jeremiah held my arm and walked with me.

Aubrey also honored his father with a fitting tribute during the funeral: "Someone's Watching Over Me." He talked about how he and his father had made peace one evening in William's hospital room. "My dad said, be who you are son. Life is not about finding yourself. Life is about creating yourself." Complete healing in that room. That's the kind of man we buried that day. No one is one dimensional. Neither was my husband. Many times, it's the one dimensional side we focus on, because it's that side that hurts us most.

The kind of treatment my sons and I received by self proclaimed righteous Christians who were close family relations was mind boggling. To be treated so unjustly by folk who don't know the whole story of the situation that happened between my husband and me, and had nothing whatsoever to do with them, was beyond logic. Where did they learn to do that? What scripture? What holy writ? Where was their Jesus when they decided that I was not good enough to bury my own husband? They knew their brother, long before I did. They had to know that as sweet as he was, he also was mean. Quick tempered. Ill. I'm thinking they were ecstatic when we married because they no longer had to be concerned with him. Perhaps that's why they were so vengeful when we separated and during his illness and subsequent death.

I was not concerned about any of them, actually. Except my mother-in-law. A sweeter, gentler woman no one could know. She loved me through it all. We talked, often, particularly when the others weren't around. She had lived her own nightmare. She understood. The most interesting thing, not one of my in-laws ever asked me about the ordeal. Not one of them. I told my mother-in-law what had happened, in a 10-page letter, soon after William and I were reconciled. She, along with one of my sisters-in-law, Serena, and my dearest brother-in-law, Carl, never stopped treating me as family. Never. Even now my mother-in-law calls me daughter, and loves me like I am.

My other in-laws and I are cordial. Serena and I keep in touch. I refuse to put myself in a place to be abused and hurt now. My response to their presence when we are in the same proximity is to be cordial, while I address my conversation, overall, to my mother-in-law. People say you choose your friends; you cannot choose your family. So true. You cannot choose the family you are born into or in most cases marry into to a certain extent. You can make a whole new family that you choose. That is what I have chosen to do.

Unforgivingness threatened to rob my happiness. I wanted to be the victim, to hear others come to my defense as they damned my mean in-laws. I could not. William was dead. He desired peace between his family and us. I would not allow unforgivingness to cause me to get stuck, unable to move forward. I would not dishonor William's legacy to be at peace by hating his family. To hate them would be to hate my own sons, whom I loved beyond measure. I had a life ahead of me. Forgiveness was my only recourse.

We came full circle, William and I. The path to wholeness was arduous, laborious, and painful. God was in the midst of us. For only God could have walked with us through the valley of the shadow of the death of our relationship, and lead us to the still waters of forgiveness and green pastures of reconciliation. Our cup was indeed overflowing in that little room at William's mother's house during the last months of his life. Laughing. Kissing. Touching. Joking. Singing. Praying. Looking. Being. That was all God. God's favor. We had lost our way. God had not lost us. Now, we were rising from the ashes of our lives. God's favor had never left me. For that I am eternally grateful.

Each of us has that right, that possibility, to invent ourselves daily. If a person does not invent herself, she will be invented. So, to be bodacious enough to invent ourselves is wise. — Maya Angelou

CHAPTER 7

Natalia has her own residence now. She and Pebbles are forging a path for themselves as mother and daughter in a large city six hours away, in the coastal region of North Carolina. I think of Natalia often. Her need to be the protector of the family, particularly of her little brother. She was like a pit bull when she felt Aubrey was being bullied or threatened. She also must have known early on that Aubrey would need extra tender loving care, that he was different. When I think back, it seems she had always come to his rescue, even when he didn't need it. Aubrey was not provocative, but he was able to hold his own. His defense was mostly words. Like me, Aubrey commandeered an extensive vocabulary. Sometimes, talk is not enough, however.

There were several incidents when Natalia was ready to go to battle for Aubrey. We were on our way to a small town outside Winston-Salem, North Carolina. I was to be the guest preacher. Natalia was driving. I was in the front passenger seat; William was in the back seat along with Aubrey and Austin. What was the discussion? It seems that Aubrey was singing maybe, who knows! Whatever was going on, William became quite disgruntled. Threatened Aubrey. I stepped in of course. I always did, in my way. My intention was to defuse the tension. I was on my way to lead worship in an unfamiliar church setting. Silence and peace were what I needed.

William did not relent. "Turn around in that seat," he said to me. "I don't need your mouth back here in this." "I have to preach, William," I responded. "This tension is making me anxious. Aubrey, what is going on?" Aubrey remained silent. I looked at his face through the rear view mirror. An ache gripped my heart. "Keep your mouth out of this. I don't need you to baby that boy. That's what's wrong with him now," William rejoined. It was then that Natalia interjected. "You don't need to be bothering my little brother like that. Why don't you just leave him alone?" Oh my. The friction that was always lying right under the surface when those two got in a conversation was flammable. "Natalia, just drive," I said. "William, please. Just let the boy alone." "Turn around and mind your business," William responded. "You don't have a damn thing to do with this."

William made a move to raise his hand at Aubrey. I don't think he had planned to hit him. Still. Both Natalia and I saw the move from the mirror. She pulled over. Came around to Aubrey's side of the car, pulled him out, and told William not to put his hands on her little brother. "I'll put my hands on him and you too if you don't get out of my damn face." Natalia bristled, bursting with adrenaline. By this time, William had gotten out of the car. There we were on the side of the road. A couple of cars rode by and blew at us, people we knew. They had no idea what was happening.

Natalia and William went around and around, neither of them backing down. 'I'm not going to that church. Just leave me right here," William stated. Once again, his nose flared in the way a skittish mare would flare its nostrils. "William," I stated. "I have to go. I'll be late." "Get the hell on then," he said. "Ok. Get in the car Aubrey and Austin. Come on, Natalia. I need you to drive." I don't think we heard a peep from Austin. In most of those instances, as I recall now, we never did. Austin did not get involved in family skirmishes. This might explain why he sometimes acted out in school. We got in the car and left William walking back towards Charlotte. Natalia is indeed a mother hen. She is the same way with her own daughter, Pebbles. It's a joy to see them together.

Austin served a few years in the United States Army, and is now studying aeronautic engineering at Sparta School of Engineering in

Oklahoma. He was married for a brief time; but is now divorced. "Dads do a number on their daughters," my friend Carolyn once said. Yes. Their sons also. And so do Moms. At 22, Austin still has a life time of opportunities to realize the dream he has for his life. I have said very little about these sons. Perhaps I should take a few minutes to say something about them. Austin was the crème de la crème for the Bell relatives. It could be because he was the first born son of his dad's children. Another factor to be considered was the fact that he was of light hue. Sad to say, but yes, families continue to make differences regarding skin color.

Austin knew very early that he was favored. It was manifested in every gift, every conversation, every expression of "that's my nephew" or "look at little William". The cousins wanted to hold him, even the male cousins. As both sons grew older, Austin was the one asked to play outside, or come over and watch a movie, or play a video game. Granted, some of that could have been attributed to the fact that Aubrey was not much of an outdoor kind of boy, nor did he particularly cater to "boy" kinds of horseplay. That could account for later in their lives as preteens to teens, perhaps. At age birth and beyond, Austin was favored. No doubt about it.

It was very rare that little Austin had to stand up for himself. Someone was ready and willing to punch or argue or defend him in some way. There were times that he would taunt his little brother, who was only one year two weeks his junior, and he would be jeered on by relatives. "Get 'im Austin," they'd say. "Go ahead, roll him on the floor," or other such ignorant comments. William thought it was a barrel of laughs. I didn't like it, not one bit. And neither did their sister, when she was around to witness it. Of course, as I've already stated, she was about the only one who protected Aubrey. His sister. His mother. We were both tolerated by the family anyway—outsiders. Married into the family. Not really family.

I have wondered whether these early escapades started Austin on a path of doing things to please the crowd. Aubrey rarely seemed to care whether the crowd was happy with him. Austin almost always sought favor with whomever he was with. I would notice how he would sometimes weigh his chances with William and me, deciding which one to please in any given moment. As I write, I cannot recall any one instance when Austin actually did something just for him, caring not at all what others thought. It was that way all through high school; his friends mattered more than anything. He became a soldier, a good one at that, pleasing the higher ranking officers, at the expense of his own needs. He had to be obedient of course. For Austin, the desire to please and be accepted was more fundamental.

I don't think Austin ever rocked too many boats. He was an obedient child, most of the time. Like me, he lived to keep the peace. When he got married, the pattern continued. The marriage was doomed to fail, it would seem. How often can anyone roll over and play dead when that one is so completely unhappy? As I continue to share my life in the next story, I hope also to give you bits and pieces of how my children are faring in this world. Austin's story will be worth revealing.

Aubrey is a senior at a well known University, in the mountainous terrain of North Carolina. His musical genius has already opened doors for him in ways unimaginable during those early years of turmoil. Aubrey was a fighter, a quiet one. He did not initiate conflict, many times walking away from it. Around the age of 15, Aubrey began to speak up, still quiet, yet quite firm. He never told me, but I'm sure it was about this time. Aubrey decided to accept his difference and he was quite satisfied with it. I hesitate to note his difference in these pages, only because this is my story, not Aubrey's.

"Aubrey, your brother told me you came out at school today," I said when Aubrey walked into the kitchen that fall evening. "Why did Austin do that?" he asked. 'You are my son," I replied with a gentle smile. "Don't you know how much I love you?" Aubrey's eyes welled with tears. "Mom," he said, "thank you." One day, perhaps he will choose to talk about his formative years. I have never wavered in my love for or support of this son. His difference has been apparent to me since he was about 18 months of age. My own special angel.

From the age of two, music was a major part of Aubrey's life. He was indeed a little songbird. It is true. Many people can sing. Many others are gifted. Aubrey has that umph factor one of my friends said with complete admiration, the combination of gift, genius, and grit that all who know him confirm will take him to the next level. Church choirs. Community theater. Performer. Soloist. Weddings. Sports venues. Marathons. Aubrey's gift has afforded him opportunities to soar. I could listen to him sing for hours. Goose bumps. This is what will set Aubrey apart, his gifts—not his difference.

He was not the favored cousin or nephew in many ways. When he would sing, he'd steal the spot light every single time. I'm eternally thankful for his gift, that he has it. It is my hope that the focus will be his gift, rather than his difference, as he continues to move forward on his chosen path. As a present to those who attended his high school graduation dinner, Aubrey presented each person with a CD consisting of nine songs. They were not his own writing. The recordings were most definitely his own style. The latest song he has recorded (though not for sale) is Feeling Good by Michael Buble. To live for! http://www.youtube.com/watch?v=ITS8w0e2Fg4&feature=youtu.be.

Aubrey is my son. There is a space in my heart that is reserved just for him. No. You don't know a secret that his sister and brother(s) don't know. Ah ha! A mother knows intuitively when a child will require a little extra love or care. This is the son who requires my little extra. My other children will be loved because they are normal. They will not encounter the choppy seas Aubrey will face. Yes. There is a special place in my heart reserved for this son. I have his back as long as I live. It is reassuring to know that God has granted this son favor, and that God has Aubrey's back also.

COURAGE IN ALL SEASONS, by Dian Griffin Jackson, October 25, 2007

Winds will blow

Leaves will come and go.

Humans will bask in your glory only to cast you down at the first opportunity.

You will need to bend from time to time—

To be silent when you had rather speak.

There will be those pesky insects, annoying animals who think they own you.

Many will take from you with little thought or care about how the taking affects you.

There will be many times when it seems you will have little or no control over what
happens to you.

Fall. Winter. Spring. Summer.

They will come.

And they will go.

You will experience planting and dying—growth and dormancy.

There will be times of abundance and months of scarcity.

Sometimes you will be overwhelmed with loneliness.

Other times you will be forlorn, worn, tired.

You will feel the tentacles of winter frost and ice zapping you of outer strength and beauty.

You will want to give up—to simply be done with the zig zag path your life will tread.

I've felt all these things—and more.

You are strong, my friend, like me.

You've observed my journey through the good, the hopeful, the glory days, and the
period where it seemed life had ended.

You, through me, have learned that the seasons teach us two things—

All things must pass; all things will return.

You have the courage, my friend.

Now live it.

Be who you are, fully present in each moment.

Watch your life blossom.

Bloom where you are!

CHAPTER

8

As for me, I'm the Senior Minister at a suburban community of faith in the mountains of North Carolina. Life has many twists. I want to say I have no regrets in my life. Perhaps I don't. I realize that everything one lives through creates the person one is at any given moment. I also know that there are events in my life I would not have asked or prayed for. Complex. I know that nothing is all black or white—nothing, not even God. I've often wondered how the world would be different if people discovered that, rather than being all powerful, all knowing, and all present everywhere all the time, God was learning how to be God right along with us learning to be human. Wouldn't it be exciting and wonderful to know that God is indeed a vulnerable God, willing to take risks for creation with no reassurance that creation will respond to God in positive ways! And another thing. I believe the teachings of the church are to blame for a lot of the stuff *Christians*, and I use the term loosely, endure. What I've witnessed in my life has almost made me ashamed to call myself a Christian. That's what I'm struggling with in this moment.

One thing that has remained constant for me is the gathered body at worship. There are six days in the week when I am confronted with the stark realities of life. Many times, it is difficult to feel the presence of God in the midst of life's stuff. And there are times when the busyness of my schedule is so hectic, I long for the peace that comes only from being alone in God's presence. That's what worship is for me. In that sacred space, it's God and me, Christ and me, Holy Spirit and me. In that moment, all of my senses (smelling, touching, seeing, hearing, thinking) are engaged and attuned to the One who is, the One who was, and the One who is to come.

I can forget all about myself, and the stuff of life, in that moment. In no other setting or moment am I completely focused on God. God and I become one, as Jesus and God are one. With my whole self, I offer a sacrifice of praise and thanksgiving to the God of all creation.

What I do is "right work" for me, something I've always been able to do but don't know how I've been able to do them. Pastoring. Preaching. Writing. Singing. Helping. Counseling. The time in my life and work when I felt most fully alive was the day I preached my initial sermon. It felt so right, sitting in the chancel, directly behind the sacred podium. Yet, even before that, the research for the sermon (even before learning about this at divinity school), the hours lying awake at night with visions of metaphors, similes, and illustrations dancing in my head, and the anticipation of standing before and with God's people for the first time with "a word from the Lord"—oh, how right it all felt. I was so alive. It seemed that everyone I called was just waiting to be of service, from printing the bulletin, or singing a song, to preparing and serving a scrumptious repast at the end of what turned out to be a 2.5 hour long worshipful moment.

I did not get tired or frustrated writing the sermon, or planning the event. It was exhilarating; those around me felt my passion and joy. I infected folk! Words seemed to flow onto the page, just as the rivers flow into the seas. When I stood to proclaim the gospel message, the words bubbled up and spouted forth like streams from an ever flowing river [which accounted for at least an hour of the 2.5 hours].

Never had I experienced such a profound sense of peace, of being in the right place. I knew I was doing "right work". The church was filled to overflowing—friends, colleagues, co-workers, family—people had gathered in that place to show support of my calling and to express their love. I was overwhelmed with joy, and the sense that after living my life doing so many other things, I was finally fulfilling my purpose in life. I was finally home. It felt so right.

From that moment until now, fifteen years later, I still experience that same sense of right work in my role as senior minister at a prestigious congregation in Jackson County, Clyde, North Carolina. When serving in this capacity, I am overcome with a freedom of knowing that I no longer need to value who I am or what I'm doing by what a man thinks about me. In all my relationships to date, my worth has been determined for me by the man I was with. When I walk in my calling, I never consider what any man thinks. I am bold. I am in charge. I am the woman who knows who she is, what God has called her to, and am confident that I can do this work. It is in these moments that I shine. That I become the phenomenal woman I am. Finally, even the men have to listen to me.

That has been very powerful and affirming for me. I'm no longer someone who should be seen and not heard, like when I was a little girl in my parents' house, or even as a wife in my marriages. No longer will I be hit or verbally abused when I speak my truth or express my concern. I'm the voice to be reckoned with. I admit that I feel a certain joy in that space. Ordination conferred upon me the right and the authority to do what I do. Yet, I serve with humility and purpose. It's what I've wanted with every relationship I've had. To be considered, valued, honored. Not obeyed. Not even followed with blinders on. To have the authority and right to speak, knowing that I will be heard, and yes, my opinions will be considered and weighed. Yes. That is one damned good feeling. Finally. I don't take it lightly. I cherish this work and calling God has placed on me. Some would say I am over the top with my boldness and authority. I sure hope not.

I still experience periods of doubt. Uncertainty. I'm at a crossroads in my faith. I take long walks. Exercise hard and regularly. Pursuer of truth. An avid reader. Talk even more; talking for me is like yoga for some. Saying it always helps me process and move forward. Question everything. As of late, there are times when writing sermons is a complete chore for me, not because I no longer enjoy preaching, because I have to temper my message with enough cliché's and implications to a sweet bye and bye that I simply no longer believe exist (at least not in the "Christian" teaching) that I sometimes feel like a hypocrite. I long for the day when congregations are comfortable with employing head and heart to this Christian journey. Brain power and faith! That would be an awesome combination!

As you read, perhaps you will reconsider the judgmental position you just placed on me. Perhaps you will rethink the label you assigned to me from that one statement. Or not. It is quite possible that you will pray even harder to keep me from burning in a fire pit somewhere under the ground that God has prepared for me and all the other brainy demons. Don't bother. I mean, thanks, but no thanks. I've prayed my share of prayers. If there is such a place and there is such a God who would prepare such a place, your prayers won't help me. Chances are they probably won't help you either.

Where, O death, is your victory? Where, O grave, is your sting?

— 1 Corinthians 15:55

Chapter 9

Today has been an interesting one. On my way to have a bone density test and a mammogram in a city about 100 miles away, my brain went into overdrive. Not unusual. I'm forever accused of over thinking a thing, anything... It is true. I do. For the life of me, I can't seem to stop doing it. A wonderful friend of mine often says to me, "You think yourself into the state of being in which you find yourself." She has to be correct, of course. Another very close and dear person to my heart often says, 'You bring a lot of your state of mental anguish and turmoil on yourself because you have to think too much about something rather than just taking it for what it is and letting it be." They both love me. I know they aren't saying these things to hurt me. But, I'm also thinking "why would one of my best girlfriends and the man I love with all my heart say such things to me. Don't they love me?" Sigh. Yes. I know, Malek. "It is what it is."

I've not shared much about my son, Malek, my firstborn. Perhaps this is a good place to speak of him, particularly the night of his murder. In some ways, his birth was similar to that of Jesus' circumstances. Unwed mother. Afraid. Unsure. Resolved. Like Mary, when my son was born, the hospital was full and there was not a room available for us to spend the night. I was as happy as I could be. Lying in the hallway that night, awaiting news of a room becoming available, I touched my baby, his nose, toes, fingers, hands, every part of him. How handsome he was! I began to dream about his life. What he would be when he grew up. Grainger, Malek's father, was there. He had driven me to the hospital.

I remember reflecting on Malek's birth and his ultimate murder when I first heard of the slaying of young Trayvon Martin. My mind, as it does when I'm confronted with the senseless shooting and murder of young men (and women), immediately transported me to that fateful day, February 2. I was at home in Fort Barnwell, North Carolina. It was late; 2:30 in the wee hours of the morning. I received a phone call from my daughter to inform me that my first born son and child, Malek, was at Duke Medical Center. He was dead—shot and killed while in the privacy of a friend's home with others doing what young men do—watching his favorite football team, the Carolina Panthers, lose yet another game. He was a fan, all the paraphernalia; he was dressed down in all those colors.

I think there are several emotional and spiritual dimensions to receiving such a phone call or answering a knock on the door with such news, that each Mother or parent experiences, even when it's difficult to admit to some of them--Disbelief-Horror-Pain-Guilt-Sorrow-Shame-Peace-Today. There are no particular steps or order to the entrance of these dimensions; there's not a today there's this, and by day four, one is feeling that. Additionally, the dimensions can resurface at any time—during a family meal, football game, song on the radio, or a person walking by who looks just like...

My first response was one of DISBELIEF. To be exact, I thought it was in poor taste for a joke. After all, just a few days earlier, my son had come to Charlotte to treat me to a nice steak dinner for my birthday. [I don't particularly care for steak.] And with his usual wry sense of humor, Malek had said to me," Mom, how old are you?" I laughed. And he began to add 2 + 2. He then, said, "dog Ma, we need to get you a life insurance policy!" I said to him, "No, you are the one we need to get a life insurance policy on!" Fun evening. His brothers, step father, and me. Less than five days later the call came in the night. Unreal. Malek and I had spoken just that day about some things that had been troubling him. Disbelief.

I returned the phone to its cradle, looked at my sleeping husband, wondering if I had heard correctly. He had, of course stirred a bit, but did not come fully awake until I told him what my daughter had just told me. "William," I said, shaking him awake. "What!" he asked, sitting up slowly. "Malek has been shot. He's dead," was my response. William sat up in our bed. And cried. Neither of us could imagine the horror our son must have felt, as he lay in that apartment, his life blood flowing from his body. Malek [Popcorn to many] had been shot in the back of his head, right above his neck. We couldn't imagine how anyone could just walk into another person's home with a gun (illegally obtained and certainly unregistered), make demands, and when those demands are not met, open fire on someone—just shoot them. Down. Like a lower primate. And walk away. My body began to shake at this point. HORROR. Imagination running rampant… Couldn't still the images, the pictures; couldn't silence the screams—his, as he lay I believe knowing that he was dying.

It was snowing that night. Our younger sons were asleep. William and I went to their rooms and shared this horrific news with them. A pallor pervaded our home. "Can I ride with you to the hospital, Mom?" Aubrey asked. "No, not this time son," I responded, reaching over to touch his brow. I dressed to drive to Durham. I didn't want anyone to ride with me. If I could do one thing differently today, I would have allowed my youngest son—who wanted so much to go with me to go, but at the time I thought I was shielding him from the horror and travesty of this injustice and brutality. I say injustice, not because of what police did or didn't do, because of what the killer felt it was his right to do in that moment.

I don't know how I made the 142 mile journey to Duke Medical Center. I was thankful that the roads were less travelled that night. I was even more thankful that God was at the wheel with me. God's favor is amazing! It seemed that when I prayed God sometimes did not hear or answer my prayers. "Where were you, God?" I pleaded. "Why did you let this happen?" I did not receive an answer. A calm presence enveloped me, a warmth flooded my heart with peace. The journey was surreal. It was if I was living in a vacuum, the life being sucked right out of my body. My heart constricted; breathing was difficult. I had a physical reaction as if I was just short of hiccupping sort of. Tears threatened to overwhelm me, but I remained stoic, focused, determined to make it there and see for myself that this was a nightmare, expecting to wake up any minute—breathing hard and so thankful to have been dreaming.

Not so. As I pulled into hospital emergency, the stark reality of my heartache was overwhelming. Earlier training and teaching had taught me how to respond in emergencies and the symptoms to look for when one is overcome with pain and emotional distress, but somehow the learning was not easily applied when it was ME—who needed the 12 step program. I knew why I was there at Duke at 3:30 in the morning, but the whole thing was still very much unreal. I approached the booth, and with a calmness I did not feel, blurted out to the attendant my need, all the while feeling a volcanic eruption about to take place in my head!

The journey to the morgue was like walking alone through a dark tunnel, with unidentifiable sounds and eerie shadows darting onto the landscape, and at the very end, there is hope as one sees the hint of a beacon of light. Then I saw him. My son. Malek. He looked so peaceful; an oxygen tube in his nose was the only evidence of any trauma. I stood back from him for a few minutes—pain, anger, sadness, disbelief, horror, guilt [What could I have done? What did I not do? Did I teach him right growing up? The whole thing became about me. Maybe if his daddy and I hadn't divorced? What will my family say? Will they blame me? What about the church—how will we bury my son? Will people know and understand what a fine young man he was? Why did he not just give the robber the money? Why did he have to be a hero this time? Is this my fault?]

I approached the bed where my son lay, the feeling of having the very air sucked out of my lungs. No. If only I could touch him, his mother's touch, his mother's love, he would get up. Yes, he would. This could not be. "Malek," I whispered. He was so handsome. He had had a recent hair shave. Head was smooth and bald. Sweet sideburns and mustache. Malek had my lips. With apprehension, I reached for him. Not wanting to. For surely then I'd know the truth. That he was dead. He'd be cold. He wouldn't make a face. Or look at me with that vintage

Holmes smile. He wouldn't turn his face towards me, or grab my hand, and say come on now woman!

AGONY. PAIN. HURT. GUILT. All came rushing up at once! Deep within my being, such anguish, never experienced before or since, welled up; and there was nowhere for the horrific pain to go. It was just in me—get it out. Please, O God, get it out. "There will be wailing and gnashing of teeth." The writer of Matthew's gospel surely experienced this kind of pain. This, then, is hell. As close to hell as one could possibly come. Not the other wordly sensation that has people trying to get brownie points with God. This is it. Hell. My hell. Surely, only heaven awaits after this.

Funeral preparations. House to pack. So many things to do. Listening to the things that would come from people's mouths. All the while attempting to maintain an equilibrium—when all I wanted to do was scream. I had to reach deep to find the faith I needed to believe in a presence or power greater than my own. It was this faith that gave me the strength to bury my beloved son. God surely must have had a similar out of body experience when Her son was hanging on the cross, dying. I'm certain Mary and Joseph were devastated, like Trayvon's mom; like me and all parents of murdered children.

Yes, there are moments when I experience peace—unexplainable, really. Let me assure you, no Mom who has buried a child will ever know complete peace; I'll never experience complete peace knowing that someone out there somewhere shot and killed my son, Malek; chances are, I'll never know who the perpetrator is. Writing about it, conjures so many mixed emotions and feelings. Even today, I want to scream. Right now. I want to scream. And blame someone. Anyone.

Throughout the entire ordeal (continuing to this day), I never knew complete peace. Once again, I had to search my heart and find a way to offer and receive forgiveness, for and from the murderer, my ex-husband, church, country, world, family, friends, MY SON. FINALLY - MYSELF. Sybil Fulton will need to find a way to forgive also. Not for the sake of the murderer, for her son, and for herself. She (nor any of us who grieve) can afford to allow unforgiveness, bitterness, and hatred to cloud our thinking and rob our spirits and lives of the fullness of God.

As I watched Sybil Fulton on the witness stand during the trial, I wanted to reach out to her, to hug her, to tell her that there are those of us who feel her anguish, share her pain and guilt. Those who are praying for her—those who know that this horror will be with her for the rest of her life. I wanted to let her know that every emotion and spiritual wrestling she was experiencing were all good—to experience them without guilt or shame.

I wanted to scream at the judge and prosecutor and defense attorney for putting this hurting, confused, unsure, horrified, scared, mother in the position to have to stand naked before the whole world and convince us that her son's life had value, that he was worth something—to someone, to her; that this son was also a child of God who deserved every protection under the law. Looking at this mother, I felt that once again justice was not being served, and that another African American mother had to bury her son for two reasons: someone decided he was in the wrong place and that person was carrying a gun with or without intent to kill, that was used to snuff out this son's life. Just like blowing out a candle, in the twinkling of an eye—another life is lost to us FOREVER. Just because... I was overcome with raw anguish as I asked the world one question: How many more mothers will have to bury their sons (and daughters) just because... ?

It is easy for others to judge Trayvon's mother, me, and our sons. Don't. We've already judged ourselves and have been found guilty. What we need, what I need, are prayers. While you're praying, pray for our leaders. Pray for our world. Let the peace of Christ dwell in you richly. Teach your sons and daughters to respect themselves first, and to respect and love others, for we are all God's family. Only then, will our sons and daughters be allowed to grow up in a world without violence and senseless murders—only then will Mothers (and fathers) no longer have to bury their sons. Finally, be gentle with a Mom (or Dad) who has had to bury a son (child) for any reason, but particularly when that child's life was taken randomly and senselessly. There is nothing that can heal the gaping, raw wound my son's murder left with me. I can only say that once again the favor of God was with me, and slowly but surely, I began to rise.

Each day I long so much to see the true teacher. And each time at dusk when I open the cabin door and empty the teapot, I think I know where (s)he is: west of us, in the forest. — [The One Who is At Home, Francisco Albanez.] English translation, Robert W. Bly©. Addition of (s) is that of the author, because the story is about a woman)

CHAPTER

10

Thoughts were convoluting my brain, overflowing into my heart, and spilling out in my actions as I traveled down I-26 on my way home today. I needed time to process them. I decided that I could not return home just yet. "Hello Deacon," I said when he answered on the first ring. "Fine, thank you," he responded as he most often did without my asking him how he was doing. "I'm calling to ask you to teach Food for the Journey tonight. I know it's a late notice. I need your help. I'm out of town." I could hear the hesitation in his voice. "Well," he began. "You don't have to teach our current curriculum, Deacon," I interjected. "You are free to choose a lesson with which you're familiar." "Alright then," he said. "Take care of yourself and we'll see you soon." "And you, Deacon," I responded. "Thank you."

About ten miles later, I directed my trusted Denali into the lush, green foliage at one of my sacred spaces, a place that the new love of my life had introduced me to last summer. It is a lovely park, off the beaten path. Changing out of my professional doctor visit attire into my lazy spring afternoon gear, I grabbed laptop, bottle of water, blanket, pillow, and cell phone (most important item of course) and entered an oasis of lush green trees and foliage. The sun was bright in the early afternoon sky, sending warm rays of hope into a desolate place in my heart that felt bereft and cold with unresolved despair. Butterflies flickered here and there, not with the bright coat of many colors they usually adorn, but their beauty was not diminished by this fact. It did cross my mind to wonder where the colorful ones were, however.

As I traversed the path to my part of the park, I listened for the song of the crickets, feeling certain that they were chirping in three-part harmony. How magical! It occurred to me in that moment that nature knew something about God, the Creator, that we humans just don't get. Even the honking of the geese added the treble cleft to the splendor of the praise! I was so touched and honored to be given the opportunity to hear, as nature joined in a wondrous chorus of praise to Elohim, that name ascribed to God when referring to God as the God of everything. As I sat up my tent near the tranquil lake, I marveled once again at the beauty of nature and offered my own form of praise in the word of the Psalmist: "Oh God, our God, how excellent is your name in all the earth." This oasis had become my sanctuary.

Looking across the darkness of the lake, watching the ripples of the waves, I began to reflect once again on the life I had lived with my husband, William. Somehow, everything always comes back to that time for me. All 16 years, 18 if I include the first eight months of separation and court battle. What went wrong, or was it all wrong from the start? Why could we not resolve our difficulties? After all, he was a child of God, as was I. He walked out of my life, not of his own choosing no doubt, but it was his choice to curse me in a vile way, to speak words of damnation on my whole future. How can one confess undying love to a person in one breath and damning curses on that same person in the next moment?

The deep, murky waters of the lake mirrored the hollow ravines of my heart. On the surface, all was tranquil. Underneath, in the depths, a cold stream flowed that felt like it would never be warmed again. I could tell you more about my marriage of 16 years. It is not my intent to cast William as a monster and me an angel. I am convinced that it takes two to tango, as the saying goes. I believe had William been able to accept the person I am, the person he was attracted to, the "me" who sparked his interest, we would have avoided much of the unpleasantness. But…for whatever reason, he could not accept "Me".

I contemplated whether William's inability to accept me negatively impacted my ability to believe that anyone has ever accepted and valued me, just because I'm me. I questioned whether anyone could love me, with no conditions, and be happy to be with me. Many times I've felt all alone, unsupported and misunderstood by those closest to me. In addition, I've felt a need to be strong for others, with no one to turn to when I needed that kind of caring, emotional strength to lean on.

Almost from the outset, it was as if William was determined to clip my beautiful wings. I was too free. It was not helpful that most of his friends were as backward in their thinking as cavemen. A woman was supposed to act a certain way. She was to obey her husband and keep her mouth shot. A small smile escapes my lips. Natalia would always laugh really hard whenever she heard William or any family member use "shot" for "shut." A woman was supposed to cook and clean and take care of the children, and when her man demanded it, she was supposed to let him have sex with her, regardless of how she felt or what her needs might be.

William often attempted to treat me as if I was one of our children. I was a college graduate, B.A. in Sociology. I was an honors graduate from a prestigious University with a Master of Divinity, and had begun work towards my Doctor of Ministry at another leading seminary. I was a thinker. I had opinions. I was an eloquent speaker. I was sought after to preach and teach. I served as the President of the Board of Directors in my Conference consisting of over 400 churches. I also served on the Board of Directors of a leading University in our hometown. I had studied abroad for eight weeks in the Middle East. I had spent time in Germany with a contingency from our Conference working with our sister church in the Rhineland on how we could offer each other mutual support. Granted, I was not doing all of those things when we met, but I was on my way. When I was awarded or applauded, I included him in every way imaginable. It was never just about me or I, it was always, my husband and me, William and I. Thinking on these things reminds me of the Apostle Paul's (New Testament) soliloquy in his letter to the church at Corinth. I do not brag; I am stating facts for the purpose of connecting the pieces.

William, on the other hand, barely graduated high school, earned a Barber's license, cut hair for awhile, cut down trees, worked as a cook. Shortly after we married, he began a lucrative business. Due to lack of trust and communication, we were never able to put that business on the level it could have been. Everything became a disagreement between us. We simply could not talk. It was as if William could not be satisfied to enjoy us until he had brow beat the us out of me. Scriptures instruct us not to be unequally partnered. I've thought those words were referring to not marrying someone who's faith was not the same as yours. Now, I believe it's more fundamental than that. To be married to another person who does not share the basics that make marriage work can be an albatross that will choke the life out of a marriage, whether spiritually, socially, culturally, financially, educationally—marriages prosper when the two people communicate and share fundamental understandings.

We were totally incompatible. I confess that I married William because I felt he had something to offer me (income) and I had a lot to offer him (stability, family, travel, exposure, better lifestyle). The longer we stayed together, the more obvious it became that our marriage would require a lot of love and tender care. I was willing to give this marriage my best me. It seemed he was also. Such a relationship as ours was hard work. With all the good we had between us, our life together was not enough. I could not measure UP to him; it took its toll.

Before you ask, of course there were good times. William was quite humorous. We laughed a lot. Especially in the early years. He adored his sons. Was proud of them. Enjoyed showing them off to his friends. He could make funny noises and the children adored his cartoon character sounds. And I mean he could cook the feathers from a goose! There was this fried chicken recipe he had--Yum! Some of our favorite times together were fishing near a bank; he with his poles and buckets and me with my blanket, Dr. Pepper, and a book! Our sons learned to appreciate fishing just as much as he did, well almost, particularly the oldest one.

There were many deep sea fishing trips. While they were on the boat, my mother-in-law and I were back at the ranch getting the frying pans ready for some serious cooking when they hauled that fresh catch to shore! Visiting family was always fun. Annual family reunions.

Teaching my daughter to drive. Giving her her first car. Working side by side in the church. Church bake sales! Oh my! My siblings loved William. I don't know if they fully comprehended what drove us apart. I wouldn't be surprised if, even today, they thought I was the problem. Heck! I could have been.

Something went awry. By the time our sons became teens, something had changed in our family. Those times I didn't share with many people at all. Who wanted to hear this story? To whom would I have shared if I could? And how many times would I have heard, "Well, what did you do to make that happen, Melanie?" Did I want people to know that much of my life was being lived in fear of getting hit by my own husband? For most of our friends and family, we were a golden couple. No one would understand what happened behind our closed doors. They certainly wouldn't believe that I had succumbed to living like this. Not badI! I'm told that instilling fear through violence and abuse are the trademarks of an abusive relationship. It is a proven fact. I am a living testimony to that fact.

Who could I tell that I had learned to walk on tip toe around the house. Watching the words I used. Fear of raising my voice above a certain decibel. Feeling the pulse of every situation, never knowing what would trigger his anger. Keeping our sons in their place so his anger would not be projected to them. I remember one particular incident. Shortly after William was shot, we were in the front room, Aubrey, Austin, Pebbles (about 18 months at the time), William, and me. Natalia was upstairs. That was always comforting to me. With renewed fury, William was complaining about his foot to the point that we had heard about all we could take. So, Aubrey, our youngest spoke up.

"Dad, can't you talk about something other than your foot? We already know all of that." William grabbed his crutch, aimed it, and threw it at Aubrey's head. I jumped to my feet with no thought of what William might do to me, picked up the crutch, stood over his bandaged foot with a vehemence that surprised me. "How dare you throw this crutch at my son! Don't you ever do that again, or I will take this crutch and stomp your foot with it." I was so furious. Not only had he thrown the crutch at our son, my little Pebbles was only inches away from the point where the crutch landed! Aubrey never said a word. He sat there stunned, in total disbelief and amazement! And he wore that knot on his head for months! I've often wondered if Aubrey forgave me for that fiasco. I didn't throw the crutch. I didn't retaliate in a real way, either. I did not protect my son.

William jumped up to the best of his limited ability. Not one of us moved to assist him. He then gave me a look of sheer amazement and a touch of fear, and hobbled down to our bedroom. He refused to admit at that time that there was anything wrong in his actions, blaming my son for the comments he made which resulted in William throwing the crutch. Months later, he told me he was proud of my response to the threat on our son. Proud of me! What the hell! Said he had never known me to defend myself or our children in that way.

Things were never quite the same after that incident. I was still fearful, but for once I finally realized that I had the advantage. No matter how well he healed, the thought of that damned crutch coming down on his foot was lodged in the back of his head. I know it stayed with me for the next two years. I was reminded of the words of Peter, "God has not given us the spirit of fear but of a sound mind and of power." It occurred to me that being frightened here and there is not a spirit of fear and is a natural emotion for anyone. Things can and do frighten us. A spirit of fear is living like I had lived for almost 16 years, walking on eggshells, afraid of my own shadow, keeping my voice soft and gentle for fear of angering this other human being to the point of causing him to retaliate in violence. A spirit of fear is a constant, daily, state of being afraid. That's how I had been living. I realized that day that God had not given me that spirit. Christians would say this fear was from the devil. I'll say that this fear stemmed from my childhood, watching my mother do what I was now doing, and seeing my father beat her anyway. It was a psychological defense mechanism I had built because I believed it was the only thing I could do.

When I stood up and picked up that crutch, I realized that God had given me a sound mind, common sense, and I did not have to let any man keep me from living fully and wholly as a created person in God's own image. I knew what David meant when he said: "no weapon formed against me will prosper" and the prophet Joel's words, "let the weak say I am strong." The words of the Psalmist that says God will make your enemies your footstool, well, that truth bears to light here also. William had slowly become my enemy. We both knew it in that moment. Standing over him with that weapon of destruction, poised to use it in the twinkling of an eye, well, William had to know that there would no longer be business as usual.

Indeed, something shifted for me that day. And for William. He saw it. He sensed it. His words no longer goaded me in the way they had for years. One day he was all out of sorts for some minor something. I don't even remember what, maybe the color of the dishes we used for dinner that night. It never took much. I was standing at the refrigerator. Our sons were preparing their plates for dinner. I had not responded to his outrage in the way he expected. I felt him before I heard him come close in my space, menacing, threatening. Aubrey was aghast. Austin just came closer to where we were standing. "I know you think I'm scared of you because you picked up this crutch that day, but I'll knock the hell out of you!" William was completely out of touch with reality. Perhaps his foot was bothering him again. The pain would flare up on occasion.

I slowly turned to face him. As I looked into his eyes, I saw a man who once had been strong and menacing, now preying on the small and what he considered helpless. I really felt sorry for him. Throughout his life he had seen his father abuse his mother and she became completely docile. Now it was his turn to be the bully in his home. That night, however, the bully was becoming the bullied. Though he still insisted on being the bully, he could no longer do so with any kind of power.

I resisted the urge to laugh. Right there. In his face. Our sons were big boys now. I knew for a fact that though they loved their father and didn't want to fight him, they certainly were not going to sit down to dinner while he attempted to beat me. Of course, I wasn't going to stand for it either. With a compassion for him that had eluded me for some time, I said to William, "I don't know what you want, but you really should just sit down and eat. Can I get you some water or something?"

He huffed into the bedroom, cursing under his breath all the way. I realized that the power God gives us in the place of fear is the power to use what is available to fight it. God gives us wisdom, sound mind, to know where and what the power is. Twice in only a few months, I had listened to the inner voice within me (Parker Palmer, Inner Teacher, Circle of Trust, 2006©), and both times, power and sound mind, replaced fear, and the outcome was celebratory.

Later that night, as I prepared for bed, William startled me with these words. "I ought to kill everyone in this house." Low. Guttural. Mean. Resigned. His lips had stretched far from his teeth, much like a horse when it is frightened. "What did you say?" I asked. "I'm hearing voices telling me to kill all y'all," he said. "William," I began. "Voices are telling you to kill your sons, and my little 18-month old Pebbles upstairs?" "I don't know. Maybe not my sons. Good thing I no longer have my gun in this shit. I'd kill all you dumb asses." With a courage I did not feel but knew I had to display, I said my prayers and turned off the lights. As I succumbed to much needed rest, my last thought was, "Yes, a good thing he no longer had his gun in this 'shit'. Good thing for him."

[31] What can we say about all this? If God is on our side, can anyone be against us? [32] God did not keep back his own Son, but he gave him for us. If God did this, won't he freely give us everything else? [33] If God says his chosen ones are acceptable to him, can anyone bring charges against them? [34] Or can anyone condemn them? No indeed! Christ died and was raised to life, and now he is at God's right side, speaking to him for us. Romans 8:31-34

CHAPTER 11

As the sun set over the lake, the extreme brightness of the sharp rays caught my attention. How long had I sat here remembering the hurt, the pain? Where were the good days? I shielded my eyes from the heat of the sun's rays as they reflected on the water by placing an umbrella between us. Not wanting to leave, though dusk was approaching, I began to reflect on one important concern. My relationships with the men in my life were more a replicable of my parent's relationship than I ever thought possible. Psychologist would call this repetition compulsion, continued repetition of choices in relationships that mirror an earlier incident in one's life. This revelation has taken me off guard. It was unexpected. Try as I might, I cannot deny the truth of it.

I've loved three men; I've been in love with two of them. The first one was a high school sweetheart. We later married and had two children. Let me rephrase that. We later married, but our first son was born before we were married legally or our union was blessed in the eyes of the church. Malek was almost two when good church folk felt Grainger and I could now receive the blessings of God's people in Christ's church. That's when we stood before the preacher in the back woods of Fort Barnwell and said "yes, we do, we sure do." Now we had permission to love, have sex, fight, have more sex, have more children. A little cynical you might say? Humm. Until then, I was a slut, Grainger a saint, and our son, unlike Mary's child, was never considered to be the incarnate word of God.

I was remembering Ms. Celie's words in the Color Purple by Oprah Winfrey©, "All my life I've had to fight. I love Harpo; God knows I do. But I'll kill him dead before I let him beat me." These are really my words when it comes to my love affair with the Church. All my life, for as long as I can remember, I have found many of the teachings of the church to be oppressive. I love the church; God knows I do. I refuse to let the church keep me in bondage. I will fight with every ounce of spiritual, physical, and intellectual strength I have if I feel that the teachings are erroneous and life debilitating. The words of John's gospel occurred to me, "I came that you might have life, abundant life." Right at the moment these words spoke life to my state of mind, a shrill voice cried out from across the water: 'Get your goddam ass over here! What the hell are you doing!" Violence. Who knows I'm here? I looked across the lake towards the sound of that voice.

My skin crawled. The inside of my stomach knotted. A flashback to my past, as a little girl and in my marriage to William (though he was particular not to use the gd word) swept me back to those times of immense anguish, pain, and yes, fear. I felt my entire body crawl into my skin, hoping to find a shield from this unexpected attack. Amazing what triggers deeply buried emotions and responses in a person. What in the world! Who would be so obtuse? In a park with children, teenagers, young families, and that's what you do? For real! That was my cue to pack my belongings and return home. The revelry was broken. I realized that the voice was not directed towards me, yet, I owned it.

My tranquil evening had become a nightmare at dusk. I could only look around as I walked at a brisk pace from the park. Flight. My senses were on high alert. I felt a keen need to escape the owner of that harsh, screeching voice who had uttered such obscenity into this lovely sanctuary. My oasis was stolen in that one brief interlude. It had been a place to come in the midst of the storm, a place to think, to write, or just to be. Surely there must be a law against this kind of inconsiderate intrusion in a public place. No such law is on the books in North Carolina. Amazing. There is a law against praying in schools. No such law against this kind of extreme disregard for others. Freedom of speech. A most necessary evil.

As I backed out of the parking lot, my revelry resumed. At 16, I fell completely for Grainger. In retrospect, I realize that my first serious crush was neither a match made in heaven, nor should it have been made on earth. We both know it now. I think even back then, Grainger knew it. We grew up in the Pentecostal Holiness Church. I thought I was a good girl, loved by God and the church. It was at church I found a place to call my own. I was more home there than any other place in my little world. At church, I was respected, admired, loved. I felt that I was valued and that my voice was heard. This was a wonderful thing for a precocious young girl like me, who had very little voice in any other setting. To be truthful, I had not been the favorite, not even at church. I was loved, but others always came before me. Or so it seemed.

I was very talented. Young people would call me a "triple threat" today: Intelligent. Eloquent speaker. Soloist. I was good too. Grainger was decent also. Not quite a triple threat; he wasn't a soloist. His grades were okay; he was mainly interested in sports: basketball and football. Church folk called him a spoiled brat. Many others called him a Mama's Boy. His Mother was a minister and he got the best parts in plays and the treatment of a favored child.

I don't know. I just thought he was kind of cute. But you know what, I don't even think I knew what "cute" was. What I knew was that I wanted a boyfriend. All the other church girls had one. I don't think I particularly cared what he looked like, well maybe a little. I had talked to boys before but that wasn't enough. If I could get a boy like Grainger to like me, I would be the envy of some of the other girls. Grainger had already been boyfriend to two of them. Seemed like it was my turn.

I went after him. I was embarrassed. It didn't stop me. I've never lacked for initiative. I wasn't the prettiest of the church girls. Short, tight hair. Amblyopia - lazy eye. Glasses. Beautiful complexion. Nice figure. Only 5'2." 110 lbs. Great voice. Had some things going for me. But my physical beauty was not up to some of the others, or so I was told. Looking at them now, well, maybe that was just not true, even then. I had a complex by then however.

Family members often called me the runt of my parent's litter. All my sisters had long, dark, gorgeous hair. They would wear the pony tails while I could only manage a pig tail here and there on my head. They were all taller. There were seven girls; six boys. I was in the middle of the bunch. Invisible. Neither the oldest nor the youngest. I was academically smart. Athletic. As a little girl, I wanted to run track. I was a cheerleader for our high school football team. Played dodge ball. Who knew? Who cared? I don't recall ever feeling completely cared for in my family, as if something was very special about me. I certainly never recall my parents attending any game, or even coming to the school except when I was in trouble. My dad didn't come even then. I was always getting in trouble, not because I did something, but because the older ones said I did, or because I was one of the bunch who simply couldn't learn to just be quiet when I knew something was not right, or the grownups were wrong.

I would have been able to understand the discipline if it was logical. But most of the time, I really was right when I pointed these things out. But, isn't it somewhere in the Bible that a child should be seen and not heard? If not, that's the way it was taught at my house. I was determined to be heard. Why should I be silenced just because the old folk said so? I remember telling my mother once that I wish I could have called Social Services or somebody when I was little because she just beat me all the time, just because. Strange, she thought that was the funniest thing she'd ever heard. I didn't. I don't think my mother ever realized how she traumatized me.

I know my dad neither realized nor cared how his beatings of my mother sent my psyche into serious overdrive and malnutrition. Yes, malnutrition of the brain. Under nourishment of the heart. Starved for comfort. Love. Hoping that someone would take my side on occasion. I can't even describe the way I felt most of the time during my growing up years. One thing I do remember. I grew up seeing that a man could do whatever he wanted to a woman and she better not say anything, or he'd just do it all again. That's in the Bible also, right?

Let me see. "Wife, obey your husband. Slave obey your masters. Men love your wife." Where does the part about "beating" her if she does not obey come in? And if it's not there, why did so many preachers and ministers of the good news condone this kind of behavior? Because they most certainly did. And the women did also. Dang! Dang! Danggit! Maybe that's the part where women were considered chattel and everyone knows that the owner could beat property and animals. Except, that's not scriptural. God gave humankind (male and female) dominion over the earth but that did not mean they were to abuse what God had gifted. Good stewardship is taking care of what God has given. Dominion is using our God-given creative abilities to make the world a haven and sanctuary for the good of all, creatures, plants, insects, humankind, you name it. Loving what God has given is not beating it down and destroying; rather, it s building up, preserving, protecting. If I knew these kinds of things as a child, why couldn't the grownups get it? That's why I'd get beatings sometimes. I challenged the status quo. And as a child, how dare I do such? Remember. I'm the precocious one!

I decided that Grainger was the man for me. Little did I know the kind of man Grainger would become, at least in the early years of adulthood. I wasn't thinking we would get married the next month or anything, though, as love struck as I was, maybe that was the hope. I admit that when I put my mind to something, I go after it with my wholeheart. Grainger and I started dating almost as soon as I made my move. From the beginning, Grainger never seemed as crazy about me as I would act like I was towards him. I took it all in stride. I had seen how my dad acted towards my mom and knew how crazy she was about him. That was just the way of men, I surmised in my little teenage brain. Yes, I was on point about many things. But the ways of things between a man and woman (boy and girl at that time) were a mystery.

At 16, dating was out of the question in my parent's house. We were not allowed to "go out". Grainger and I courted in the back of the church, and in the backseat of the pastor's station wagon on the way to some church function. We enjoyed sitting in the very back. Don't play. You know why! We could feel each other. That's what the boys and girls did. I have no clue why we were never caught. It would get pretty raunchy in the hatchback part of our Pastor's old station wagon. It was a French mustard yellow color. Ugly. We didn't mind. It would get really quiet during some points of our drive. Pastor would say, "ya'll awake back there; mighty quiet." "Yes ma'am. We're awake." It used to startle us in the beginning; we thought we had been caught. But of course, as only the very young can do, we quickly realized that she was none the wiser to our meanderings. We didn't do any heavy duty necking and pecking, you understand. Just a sneak feel. It took me awhile to let Grainger touch me. "Grainger," I would say, "you know we aren't suppose to do that. God wouldn't like us to do that. We're saved." "I know, baby," as he continued to touch newly budding nipples which though a little painful, still felt good, or as his fingers snaked under my skirt to a very sensitive spot on my thigh. Come on. Who could fight City Hall? Right?

So. Of course. When he was old enough to get his license and drive a car without parental supervision, the first time we had a chance to be alone? Damned spiffy! We took that petting to a whole new level. We were on our way to some church function. Grainger was driving his mother's tan Oldsmobile. We pulled over alongside the road, near an abandoned building. Giggling as we moved to the back seat, Grainger was very sweet and helpful. "Are you okay," he asked with the chivalry of a 16 year old. "Yes," I replied, as demur and nervous as it was possible to be.

We began touching each other. Kissing. In ways never before. I remember thinking it felt just so sweet. Good. His hands were everywhere. He instructed me to touch him here and there, and to open my mouth like this and that when we kissed. I remember it was raining that night. At one point, I looked at our bodies, which by then were scarcely clothed. I saw these designs on our bodies that frightened me. "Grainger," I said, "oh my god, something is wrong. Look!" The thought crossed my mind, oh my, now everyone will know what we've been doing. We've got the marks to prove it. Suddenly Grainger began to laugh. "Girl," he said, "that's nothing but the shadows of the raindrops on our skin."

We laughed. I felt like a complete idiot after he proved that's what it was. I remember feeling a profound relief that no one would know what we had been doing it. We were awkward in that back seat, but I had the distinct impression that Grainger had a little more experience than I did because he seemed to have the general idea of what we were supposed to be doing. It never crossed my mind to question him about anything. I just went with the flow.

I was expecting more of what we had done in the backseat of our pastor's car. When Grainger removed my panty I was shocked at the way I was feeling, and the response of my body to his touch. I had responded the other times, but this was different. He looked so handsome to me through the rain in the moonlight. It was a beautiful night. Everything just felt so right. There was pain. He was so gentle, rushing but not frenzied. I did not fight. I lay back. And he loved me. Young love. First love. It's like that. I felt a forever kind of feeling.

We did not go out again like that for months. Shortly after our love nest that moonlit night, I discovered that I was pregnant. At eighteen, and a freshman in college, I was about to become a mom. I did not tell anyone at first, not even Grainger. When I did tell him about the baby, he was appalled. "Are you sure it's mine!" he asked. Of course I was sure. He had been my first and only lover. He didn't want to hear that. He was still a senior in high school. A jock no less. The girls loved him. That was when I first realized that he was a boy, what women sometimes call a "Momma's boy." And when I knew for certain that sex was not about love for him. Grainger was certainly not interested in being married. It was hard for us to believe that I could be pregnant after the "first time." We were scared. I was numb. I returned to my second semester of college in a euphoria, not of joy. I knew that Grainger did not want our child, and possibly not even me.

But I'll give credit to those little old mothers in the church. Our secret was soon discovered. What's the Biblical phrase: "Be sure your sins will find you out" and the wives tale, "what you do in the dark will come to the light?" The foreboding I felt that night in the backseat of that Oldsmobile was now being fulfilled. The church called our love "sin." I never did. I still don't. We had fornicated, they said. Granted, our love had not been condoned and approved by the church in a ceremony. I would never think of the love we shared as something evil, ugly, dirty. And I certainly could never accept that our baby was a mistake. The church stripped us of our positions of leadership, made us come before the whole assembly and apologize, for having sexual relations and particularly because I was pregnant. That has never set right within my heart or mind, certainly not within my spiritual heart. I had given myself to the man I loved, freely. We produced a beautiful little boy. And the church condemned us. I grew and regressed simultaneously in that moment.

Out beyond ideas of wrong doing and right doing there is a field. I'll meet you there. When the soul lies down in that grass the world is too full to talk about. – Rumi

CHAPTER 12

I've observed many "sinful" acts in the church. Pastors shunning my pastor because she was a woman. Husbands abusing wives and the church turning its head. Choir members fussing and fighting about who could sing and would sing what song. Ugly words between church leaders. Some married folk, even preachers, sleeping with persons not their spouses. I had seen these kinds of things. Children ignored: unbathed and unkempt. I had seen so many things that surely must have been the real sins. What Grainger and I had between us was love. How could love be a sin? There is a verse somewhere in the Bible that says God is love. Then, if that is so, God must know all about love, right? How then, can the church, acting as God's emissary, call what Grainger and I had between us, sin?

I still ask that, though no longer with confusion. I ask it with regret that the church condemns so much that is right and permit so much that is wrong. The good news for me is that over the years, I've matured in faith and scripture and have learned that to take the Bible seriously, many times means it can't be taken literally. I stand by that. In my view, if God did not send Jesus to condemn but to save, then what right does anyone have to condemn me? Let me see, back to the Bible again. "The one whom the Son sets free is free indeed!" I thank God for setting me free, for delivering me from the bondage of narrow minded thinking, acting, believing, and doing.

Some would say, "Pastor, you are promoting illicit sexual promiscuity and behavior which the Bible clearly speaks against." My response. "No. I am saying that love comes in many forms and ways. The church has no right to interfere with my way of expressing love that is consensual between two mature persons who are not hurting or dishonoring another sacred covenant or each other because of the lack of an official or legal covenant." I do not believe that God wants people to live in bondage to anything, not even church dogma if it teaches one to be a prisoner. No. I do not support promiscuity. There has to be boundaries, of course, or we would become just a passel of animals, rutting around in the ditch with whomever and whatever. I do promote love. And I'm in favor of the sexual expression of that love. It is my conviction that sexual love should only happen between two consenting persons who are of age and understand the ramifications of the act. There are extenuating circumstances that can contribute to preventing adults from getting married in the eyes of the church. I question whether these reasons hinder their commitment to each other in the eyes of God. I do not condone adultery.

When I reflect on these things, I would add to this conversation that the primary reason the church is especially anti-same gender loving persons and other expressions of love is because the church is anti-sex. The church has difficulty considering or accepting the possibility that Mary and Joseph were husband and wife and "begat" other children after the birth of Jesus. Anything about love and sex that is fun, wonderful, beautiful, and not proscripted by the church is sinful. Which has to mean, of course that gay love is sin. Not because God says so, only because of an uninformed hermeneutic of the Bible rendered by the church. I've often wondered what folk would do if they found out Paul or Jonathan and David or Naomi and Ruth, if not gay, were at least bi! Wouldn't that be something! What was that thorn in Paul's side anyway, that needed God's unmerited grace to help him make it through his life? Who knows? But why is the church so afraid of sex, which in my way of thinking is the most beautiful expression of love God gave to humankind?

It is these kinds of questions that have plagued me all my life. Even now, as I sit at home reflecting on my marriage to Grainger, the questions still surface. And there are no concrete answers, not even in the Bible. What is in the Bible is how we should learn to love one another, not sexually, but as one family of God. Jesus was quite clear on that, though he didn't respond to a lot of today's issues. "Love God with all you are, and love your neighbor as you love yourself." Then the question becomes, how many of us love ourselves? I paraphrase, but that's what the Biblical authors did also. Actually, much of their writings are inaccurately credited to Jesus. But that's a story for another day.

When Malek was born, I was totally happy. Grainger took me to the hospital. "What's the little popcorn's name," Grainger's mother asked as soon as Grainger told her about the birth. "Malek," he responded. But don't you know that the nickname Popcorn stuck with Malek throughout his life! It was a good day. Grainger was good with Malek. He came over often in the beginning. There came the time, however, when he had reasons for not spending time with us. Driving bus after school. Football. Basketball. Homework. Didn't have a ride. It continued like this for almost two years. Grainger was moving farther and farther away from us. I believe that Grainger's mother is the reason he and I got married. Grainger had graduated high school, joined the army, been discharged, and had been to college. I had even lost one of my brothers to an accidental drowning. Much had happened in those 2.5 years.

We were married in our home church. Everyone was thrilled. The loose woman had become morally good. The bastard now had a father. And the man could hold his head up in society because he had done right towards his woman. Did anyone think that neither of us was ready for marriage? That we had no clue what we were in for? Who among those good saints thought to talk with us, openly and honestly, about marriage and all its ramifications? The only thing that mattered to the saints was appearances. So unfortunate. Our marriage was for them, so they could be proud of these young people again, who had been such pillars in the youth department. The devil meant this sinful thing for their bad but God turned it around for their good. Cliches. Why so many clichés in the church? Where are the real life issues being discussed?

After we were married, Grainger and I moved from our hometown of Fort Barnwell to what seemed to us as a metropolis, Raleigh, North

Carolina. Two years later, we were pregnant again. But this time, Grainger was adamant that he did not want another child. He even threatened to leave me if I kept our child. "This could be the daughter I've been praying for," I pleaded. "We will be fine. Everything will work out." Grainger would not budge. "I don't want another child right now. It is just not a good time," he emphasized. I could see that he was becoming more agitated as the conversation continued. "Grainger, we love each other. Our baby will have everything it needs. You'll see." My words were falling onto closed ears and a hardened heart. "I'm leaving if you keep the baby, Melanie. You decide."

As you can see, something happened between high school graduation, two years of marriage, a year and a half in the army, and one year in college. Grainger had become cold. Bitter. He began to hang with a different kind of crowd. We weren't attending church as we once did. Moving away to a large city (compared to our hometown), there were no mothers or deacons to keep us in line. Grainger started staying away from home. He became ill-tempered when he was at home, noncommunicative. Our conversations lost their gaiety. Bills. Jobs. Son. Pressures became too much for Grainger, and for me.

We did not keep the child. How could I? I loved my husband. I did not want to live without him. Aborting my child was the worst nightmare I had experienced in all of my 21 years. All these years later, to think on this low point in my life take me back to that low place. Deep. Dark. Clawing my way out. Trying to find the light again. Wanting to laugh again. All I had left were my tears, and the silence that follows having to get rid of the beautiful life within me that I believed had been made in love with the person I cared about more than anyone in the whole world. The husband who told me to lose it or lose him. The person who was supposed to love, honor, and cherish me, sent me into a dungeon filled with vipers, alone. Not even God followed me there. And no matter how hard I prayed, God neither heard nor answered me.

For once, Grainger had made all the arrangements. Amazing. This same man who could not keep a job, or make any real decisions about most things, had no problems arranging for me to abort our baby. There was a house somewhere on Elder Street near the K-Mart Shopping

Center where a woman by the name of Ms. Tippett lived. Grainger took me there. Dropped me off. Left me in the care of a woman I had never met. A woman someone had told him about. "Take off your clothes from the waist down. Put them on this chair, and follow me upstairs," she said. Distant. Cold. Business. She pointed towards this child sized bed and told me to lay down. "Put your feet in these stirrups," she continued. I began to shake. I felt so cold. Inside my heart felt as if the blood no longer flowed. Outside, my extremities reacted as if they had frost bite.

There was a basin near the foot of the bed. Lots of white cloths, like torn sheets. Instruments. Some I recognized from previous pregnancy and doctor visits. Some foreign. Once she began to work, there was very little conversation. I felt tugging between my legs. The sounds were harsh. Metal clanging. Swishing. Groping. Pain. "Go sit on the commode," she said. I did. And within minutes, amid my moans and groans of agony, a large mass left my body and fell into the commode. Ms. Tippett came in. Gave me a towel to place between my legs. Instructed me to lie down again. Attended to something in the bathroom. And then attended to me.

"Do you know what sex my baby is" I asked? My voice sounded alien, hollow. "No; it's too early to tell," she responded in a deadpan voice. After much of the bleeding had stopped, Ms. Tippett wrapped me in a large padding, gave me more to take home, and sent me away. Grainger came for me. Didn't ask about the fetus. Took me home. "Thank you," he said. And with those words, my whole life changed to such an extent I didn't even recognize myself for years. That could have been the beginning of my descent into hell. Not a day passed I didn't wonder about my child. Whether a girl or a boy. Was there much hair? The color of her eyes. At the outset of the pregnancy, I wanted a girl. Grainger never spoke about it again.

We draw our strength from the very despair in which we have been forced to live. We shall endure. — Cesar Chevaz

CHAPTER

13

Later that night, the bleeding returned. Heavy. Cramps. Pain. Fever. We went to the hospital.

"What happened sir," the nurse asked.

"I'm not sure," Grainger said. 'I think she's having a miscarriage."

"When did it begin?" The nurse continued with a barrage of questions. Finally, I gave them the whole story. By this time, the doctors knew the truth of what had happened. Ms.Tippett had not removed all the afterbirth. I had developed pregnancy poisoning, which could have developed into severe eclampsia. The doctor told my husband that I would have died had I not come into the hospital when I did. Favor. God's favor. Even in my mess. God favored me. I did not believe God either heard my prayers or cared about me, and yet God was faithful all the time. When I needed God most, God was right there. I cried and cried and cried. For all I had lost. For loving a man who didn't care to love me. And for letting him convince me to give up my unborn child. His reasons were so pathological then. And in hindsight, we lost our child for no good reason at all. My being obedient to his wishes did not change the tide for us. We were on a very slippery slope, going downhill faster than we could control. Drugs entered the picture. Not only did he begin selling drugs; he also began using them.

This was not the only time I did something that was so out of character for me just because Grainger said if I loved him and wanted our marriage to work, I would do it. He wanted to spice up our sex life, he said, and insisted that smoking a joint was the best way to do so. After much cajoling and when I had just about run out of patience, I succumbed to his request. I can say with truth here. I smoked a joint one night, in our home, with psychedelic lights flashing all over the place, it seemed. The feeling was smooth and yes, nice and peaceful. The only reason I never tried it again was because I had no control over my actions. I could not appreciate the feeling of floating beyond my ability to stop floating if I desired. "I can't do this again, Grainger," I said the next day. "It was fun," he said. "I haven't seen you laugh and have that much fun in a long time." "I know," I responded. "But I was too out of control and I didn't like it. And I felt kind of silly laughing when there was nothing to laugh about." I stopped. Grainger continued.

Two years after the abortion, I was pregnant again. There was never a question but that I would have my baby. I, of course, told Grainger about the baby. He tried to be happy. Perhaps he was. There was no discussion about whether this child would be born. I wanted a daughter. A little girl all my own. To dress up. Comb her hair. Put Vaseline© on her legs so they would shine all pretty and brown, just like mine. A little girl to cuddle, and hold, and tell girl things to. It never occurred to me that this baby would be other than a girl. And she was. Natalia. Beautiful. Sweet. She came into the world one hot August day screaming at the top of her lungs. Those soulful eyes looked right at me. She curled her finger around my own when I touched my finger to hers. I was hooked. And I was determined that her life would be better than my own, and that I would never let anyone hurt her.

Grainger was moving further and further away from me by the time Natalia was born. He was always between jobs. His personality began to change during this period. Our relationship was in a functional mode. We stayed together. He did his thing. I cared for the family, our children, the bills, everything became mine to do. To keep him from leaving me, I reframed from nagging or arguing. We were falling behind in everything. Grainger did not seem to care about these kinds of things. He was in his own little world.

My knowledge about drug addiction was still quite limited. It never occurred to me that Grainger was functioning the way he was because of his addiction. My personality is one that always gives a person the benefit of the doubt. For the next four years after Natalia's birth, I continued to pray and hope that Grainger would come to his senses and be the man I needed him to be, to care for his family, in every way. I prayed that he would see the beauty of his children and the loving support I offered him. It did not happen. Matters got worse.

One day during the drug period, we had sat down to a meal as a family. A friend of Grainger's came over. People called him Weasel. After a knock on the door, my husband looked out the kitchen window and invited Weasel in. "Come on in, Weasel," my husband seemed so excited that Weasel was there. "Come on into the kitchen. We're about to have dinner." Weasel came in, barely a nod to me or our children. Walked right up to the dinner table. Took out a plastic bag. Poured the green contents onto our table, and began measuring out the contents into several piles

I was aghast. By now, I recognized not only the appearance of the marijuana plant, also the distinct fragrance. "Grainger, you had better tell Weasel to get that mess off our table. We are having dinner." I protested. Grainger looked at me. "Oh, it will only take a few minutes," he said. He and Weasel concluded their business. Weasel left. Our son and daughter, ages five and eight, were none the wiser. I felt an acute fire in my chest akin to heart burn that was so powerful, I was certain I was about to have a heart attack. That was the beginning of my disrespect for and complete shame to call this man, husband. It also was the day my fountain of love for him dried up.

Grainger began to spend longer and longer periods of time away from home. Lost income. Months and months with no work. I continued to hold us together, working at the college, taking care of the home, and the children, and the bills. Grainger disappeared more and more. Funny thing. At first, it wasn't even another woman. Drugs. Embarrassment. Fun with the boys. Anything to keep from being reminded of his responsibility as a husband and father.

Our children and I attended a Baptist church during my marriage to Grainger. They were very active in the church. Choir. Usher. Youth Fellowship. I served as the Youth Director. We travelled to other churches and in general had a great fellowship with the young people in these churches. We excelled in the activities in which we participated and or sponsored at our own church. Our daughter, Natalia, was such an angel. Everyone loved her; she was mannerly and lovable, but this little one had eyes only for her mother. We were inseparable. There was one young lady able to steal her away from time to time, I recall. She continues to be my very best friend to this very day.

Malek, our son was a song bird. Three years Natalia's senior, he stole the show with his voice, good looks, and overall gentle and generous nature. The older folk thought he was super sweet, especially those good church mothers. We had been attending this particular church for about seven years when Grainger came to a worship service for the first time. The entire church gasped in amazement to know that I had a husband; my children a father who lived in our home. He attended once, not again.

I was not afraid of Grainger. Never had been. Partly because he had never hit me, or raised his voice in a threatening tone for the most part. I had gotten loud with him. But through our years together, thirteen of them, not once did he become irate and frightening. He simply disappeared. So. I learned to keep my voice a decibel lower than I wanted for fear that he would leave – again. I learned to keep quiet about his not working, blaming myself for his lack of concern for his children and for his lack of caring for his wife and his home.

It had to be me, didn't it? My dad often told my mother that. "If it weren't for you and all these children…." Uncanny how so much of Ben's conversations with my mother when he was in a drunken stupor sunk into my subconscious. Uncanny. In an effort to make sure my husband could never blame me for any of his mess, I turned it on myself and tried to project good qualities on him despite his trifling ways.

Life with Grainger was hard. I worried about him. A lot. I worried about our children. I worried about what would happen if he left one day and never returned. I worried about why I remained in a marriage where it was obvious to everyone, and to me, that Grainger certainly had no desire to be a part of it. At one point, I became deftly ill. My hands stopped working. It became increasingly difficult for me to drive, do chores around the house, even accomplish the requirements of my job, as an Administrative Supervisor for a large teaching hospital.

After several tests, including a liver biopsy, stress test, and a lot of blood work, doctors finally decided I had Sarcoidosis. It was not so. One day, during one of my follow ups to the myriad tests, a Physician Assistant asked me about my life. A few minutes into the conversation, my diagnosis was apparent, and so was the solution. Stress and strain of being married to a man who did not want to be married to me or anyone for that matter, was killing me. Yet, I stayed. Why?

All the most powerful emotions come from chaos—fear, anger, love—especially love. Love is chaos itself. Think about it. Love makes no sense. It shakes you up and spins you around. And then, eventually, it falls apart. – Kristen Miller

The church told me that if I were to leave my marriage, I'd be condemned to a life without love, touch, intimacy, or romance. After all, God (no, make that Jesus, but then they are the same in the teachings of the church, right?) said that if I divorced for any reason except my husband committed adultery, then I couldn't love again, have sex, or remarry because then I would be committing adultery. In hell I would lift up my eyes. Total ignorance to my way of thinking. I was in the minority.

At the time, I wanted the church to love me and think I was great. That way, I would feel that God also loved me, and that God would think I was super duper. That was my cross to bear, right? No cross, no crown. Women, obey your husband in the Lord for this is right. Damn. Oh my goodness. Damn. Damn. Damn. If only I could see some of those folk who made me live in hell just to die and go to hell, since I would never be saved enough for heaven anyway.

There were times when my children were hungry, or needed shoes, or just school supplies. My salary barely paid the bills, though I made an equitable wage. Often there was never enough left for groceries, clothing, shoes, school supplies or other school or church activities. "Grainger," I would say on many occasions, "when do you think you will get a job? The children need…" whatever the need might be. "Well you might need to get a second job," he'd respond. "I'm doing the best I can." After these conversations, he would go away.

There were men willing to help me. But they all seemed to want more than i could ever give them. I loved Grainger. My body was his to love and him alone. There came a day, however, when I did choose to be a friend to this one man who in turn befriended my family. I remember once telling Grainger that we needed food. "Go get some then," he responded, without even looking up at me. That night, I left the house. Made a phone call. Returned home a couple of hours later with a complete meal from Kentucky Fried Chicken.

Grainger sat down to the table and ate as if he had brought us that meal. I was so damned angry. Literally, I exploded. "How on earth can you sit down and eat that chicken knowing you did nothing to get food in this house," I yelled! "Well, it's in here isn't it? If food comes in this house, I'm going to eat it," he said, smacking his greasy, well endowed lips. "You want to know where this food came from?" I asked even more belligerent than before. "I saw that man pick you up down at the corner. When you walked out of the house, I followed you," he replied, without blinking an eye or pausing between chews.

Calm as a lazy summer breeze. Content as a pig in slop. Every nerve in my body screamed with anger, hurt, disappointment, and loss. I could not believe this man. I could not believe that he sat at that table, ate the food as if it was finger licking good, and gloated about knowing that I had to give myself to some dude for our children to eat, and, what, that was alright with him. That's what our family had come to! My defense mechanism triggered into overdrive. A calmness spread over me for the first time in years.

A few weeks after that night, Kenneth, the man who bought the food for us, died. A freak death actually. He had gone into the hospital for hernia surgery. Died in recovery. I didn't mention it to Grainger, of course. On the day of Kenneth's funeral, Grainger made one of his infrequent trips home." You know Kenneth died, don't you"? I felt the hairs rise on the back of my neck . Of course I knew he had died. We worked together. The funeral was that day. "Well, just so you know. I had that N---- killed," he said. His words grabbed at the core of my being. "Yeah," he continued. "I went to one of my friends in South Carolina. Took her that baseball cap you had on the bureau dresser. She worked a root on him. Didn't everyone think it was weird that he died from such a simple surgery?" I could only stare at the stranger who sat across from me.

Grainger sat at the table with a look of complete satisfaction. Again, calm as an ocean breeze. I was mesmerized. As I continued to stare at him, I did everything I could to see something of the man that I had loved so deeply for 13 years. I knew in that moment all the love was gone. Gone. I hated him. Not because of what he just said. I didn't believe in that stuff anyway. Plus. I knew that sometimes simple surgeries can become complex, depending on other conditions in the body.

But for him to sit in front of me, and tell me this, as if he was discussing the weather or a trip with the children to the park! I had degraded my body and lost my self worth in my attempt to provide for my family. I loathed Grainger then. I had been prepared to work with him, do whatever we could to rebuild our family. As I sat there and looked at him, I simply detested this man. And I knew if I sat there much longer, I would hurt him. "I'll tell you what," I said, with a peacefulness that had eluded me for years, "you are crazy. But let me help you out. Here you are. Take this piece of my hair and take it to your root working friend in South Carolina." I was adamant. "Better yet, take my underwear, Grainger," I offered with a sneer, as I yanked them down around my legs. "If you think you're scaring me, you have one more think coming. I'm not afraid of any root worker; and I'm not afraid of you. I'm leaving you. I want you out of this house. But not to worry. You don't have to go. I'm leaving."

He didn't blink an eye. He never asked me not to go. He showed no reaction to my declaration whatsoever. With those words, I stood up, looked at him one last time, walked out of the house, got in my car, and went straight to a realtor. He went to wherever he goes in those long periods from home.

I found a condominium a few weeks after that conversation. A couple of days later, I returned to our home to collect a few household furnishings. As I approached the door to place my key in the lock, I noticed a commotion at my daughter's bedroom window. With a degree of hesitancy, I knocked before inserting my key. No answer. I turned the key in the lock, walked inside. Grainger had been gone for some time. Yet it was obvious that someone was inside our house.

I called out. "Hello?" A slight stirring down the hall. I walked in the direction of the commotion. Children. Startled, I asked who they were. All four voices piped up with names, I do not recall. "Who is here with you? Is your mother here?" A young girl, maybe about thirteen, said her mom was in the back room. Grainger and my bedroom. I asked her to get her mom, please, and she complied. I didn't know it then, but within a year, the young girl I spoke with, would become the mother of my first grandson. The mother came to the front of the house. "I'm Melanie Carey," I said. "And you are?" "I'm Grainger's girlfriend." I was flabbergasted.

I looked at this woman and those children. I could not wrap my head around the fact that a man with his own beautiful son and daughter would abandon them to move in a woman with four strange children into our home. By this time, I should not have been amazed by anything Grainger Eugene Carey did. "I've come to collect a few things that I left here when I moved. It will only take a few minutes," I said.

Turning, I walked through the dining room into the kitchen and collected just a few kitchen items. I then walked down the hallway and collected a few bathroom supplies. The little eyes followed me as I walked. The girlfriend sat down in the living room. This entire process took less than 15 minutes. As I walked to the front door, I turned to Grainger's girlfriend. "Here is your key," I said. "I will not need it anymore." I then said good bye to the children, and to the woman my husband had moved into our home. Deborah, she had said. Deborah. Damn. Out the door. Down the steps. Proud as a peacock. Head high. Chin up. Never looked back. Not even once. To this day.

One of the most crippling things we can do to ourselves is expect someone else to make us happy. — Sue Patton Thoele

CHAPTER
15

I had done it. The unthinkable. Certainly the unexpected. Moved into a new place with no husband and two children. The mind and body are an unified machine. The minute I made up my mind that I had to get out of this deathtrap of a marriage, I was healed. Completely. At least in body. I never needed to see another doctor about my physical condition. One thing is for certain, I did not have Sarcoidosis or any known disease. I was heartbroken. Devastated. And it took its toll on me, physically, psychologically, and spiritually. I didn't doubt there was a God during this time. I admit, in that moment, God seemed very far away.

Once the decision was made, divorcing Grainger was easier than I imagined. There is this little known fact about me. I'll fight to the finish for something if I believe in it. Once the fight is gone, it's gone. I'm ready to move on. Using the internet, first I typed up separation papers, had them notarized, and sent a copy to Grainger. He did not dispute anything. From that point, using the internet again, I typed a petition to the court filing for divorce. Pretty straightforward. Filed the papers. $50 I think. Maybe $30. The courts sent a copy to Grainger. I had removed the items I wanted from our house, which didn't amount to much since he had already moved some other woman into our home. I did not want anything in there that had now become 'theirs'. My car was already my own. We had lived apart over two years. The decree was more a formality for the State records. In every conceivable manner, Grainger and I had been divorced a long time.

Natalia was about eleven at the time her dad and I separated. For the most part, I did not receive child support from Grainger from that time until her high school graduation. When he did contribute to her care, it was a struggle. I soon decided that it was not worth chasing him down. I had to learn to manage my home on my own. With God's help, favor, I did exactly that. God always provided appropriate angels to come to my aid in the right times. In addition, I've had a professional career that provided substantial benefits and lucrative income. College really pays off! And yes, so does prayer and a whole lot of faith.

What I found most challenging was the way my self-esteem had taken a beating. By the time Grainger and I were divorced, I had met William, had a son, and had moved on in so many ways. Or so I thought. Not so. I recall receiving my divorce decree in the mail. Somehow, the finality of it shook me to my core. I had promised to love, cherish, and honor Grainger until death. I had failed. My love had been rejected. He did not want me. He did not want our children. I had not been good enough to keep him.

I remember having a serious pity party a few months after the divorce. Natalia was 14; Malek was almost 17. My new son, Austin, was one. I even had a grandson, Sherman, who was also one. I took an inventory of my life that day. I was 37. I was a University graduate with a B.A. in Sociology, a minor in English. My profession was an Executive Administrative Manager at a high ranking medical center. I lived in a 2-bedroom apartment, now, having moved from the home I owned with Grainger. I owned my own car. I had met and was loved by a man, William, with a mean temper and very little else in terms of material possessions. Malek, of course, didn't put up with any of his horse shit. When he was around, there was very little of that manure spread around either. Malek was about to graduate from high school and would be joining the navy. My apartment was decently furnished, not richly so. We dressed nicely, not overly couture.

During the inventory, I recognized that this was not all I had wanted for myself by age 37. I had plans. I would be an acclaimed writer or lawyer by this time. My children would be smart, beautiful, well cultured, off on one international adventure after the other. I would be married to a brilliant doctor or surgeon. Together, we would make our mark on the world. People would know who we were and would seek our favor. Essence and Jet would feature stories about us on their cover pages. Of course, so would Vogue, Cosmopolitan, Time. The Carey Family would be in households across America, and beyond. Instead, I'm in a second marriage, and living in a small community in Matthews, struggling to survive, one paycheck to the next.

My parents had gifted children. I was considered by my siblings to be one of the more gifted of us. Even today, they see me as not living up to my potential. What happened? Once again, I found myself with another man who was a lot like my dad in many ways. How could this happen over and over?

Continuing the self assessment, I learned one thing about me that was horrifying. I had lived my life looking for the man who would be great: greater than my dad, nicer than my dad, more loving than my dad, richer than my dad, everything better than my dad. What I had done, in each of my relations with a man, was to seek out and marry my dad. Low achievers. Insecure. Attracted to powerful women. Egocentric. Chauvinistic. Humorous. Sweet. Mean. Christian.

It's as if I had it written across my forehead: 'Looking for a man just like my dad'. My mom didn't get it right. I'd get it right for both of us. Over the course of my life, as I took inventory, that's exactly what I had done. I had settled for men just like my dad. And like my mom, I had placed the man's needs and wants far above my own, and in some cases, that of my children.

I had not placed emphasis on my career or needs in ways that mattered. In each case, I had justified what I did by saying I'm doing it for my children. I'm doing it because I love him. It was my own insecurity and doubts that kept me in the relationships. The thing is, no one would have described me as this person who was too timid to speak up for herself or would let anyone run rough shod over her. That is not the person you saw in any aspect of my life except in my relationships with the men in my life. I had a reputation for being strong, feisty, assertive. What happened to that person?

Behind closed doors, I was a passive-aggressive personality. I had very little self worth, believing that my identity was tied completely to having a man in my life. I was willing to accept the blame and guilt that I was responsible when the relationships didn't work out. That's the legacy I grew up with. It is not the legacy I desire to leave behind. As aforementioned, someone said to me once, "dads do a job on their little girls, don't they?" Well. Hell yeah!

Unconditional love is what a child should expect from a parent even though it rarely works that way. — Jeanette Winterson

Chapter 16

Once again I find myself sitting in my most favorite place to think, write, read, be. The water is quiet, as if waiting for the follies of nature to intercede and rollick its gentle course to a fevered, stormy foam. But for now, it is content to flow merrily along its crystal path embracing the swooping seagulls and ducks, whose honks lull me into serenity. This is a small piece of paradise, tucked away from the hustle and bustle of car horns, squeaking tires, and noisy pedestrians. This is where I most readily experience the presence of the Other, the life force greater than my own yet intricately interlaced with all I am. In every flutter of the butterfly, every hum of the bee, and each tap tap tap of the woodpecker, God is so present in this place

I think how simply marvelous it would be to worship here. One could sing or speak or dance or even pray at one's heart's content. No formality. No script. I can imagine the birds and the rabbits and the frogs peeking from behind every bush and lily pad and through the leaves of the trees joining in such a happy chorus of praise! It would be like "Alice in Wonderland!" So amazing! An adventure! Look! There's a duck family gliding across the lake. Well, doesn't that beat all? The parents are gay! And two seagulls dived down to welcome them! They have come to join me in worship! How phenomenally cool is that! This is my bias of course, but as I watch that little hummingbird flitting from branch to branch, it occurs to me that the flower people of the 60's or 70's might have gotten some of this right, minus the extracurricular sex and excessive stoning. Then, who am I to judge? It's not for me, but who knows that they didn't get that part right also!

Life is for living. That's on the real! To live in this world, one cannot be faint of heart. Strength is needed. Determination. Desire to live. To move forward. The psalmist who penned the phrase "One Day at a Time" obviously knew something about life. Many times, that is the only hope left to us. I don't know how I made it. Two children—a teenage son and a preteen daughter, bills, needs. People would say to me, "you're such a strong woman!" I learned to hate that particular sentiment; still do. What has strength gotten me except screwed up relationships, men who simply did not know how and cared even less about learning to appreciate and love me. Not who they wanted me to become – me, Melanie, my mother's daughter. Men who literally took my kindness for weakness and trampled me, emotionally, physically, spiritually, and psychologically—beginning with my father.

I spent a lot of my free time as a little girl growing up under the porch of our house or in an abandoned car in the back yard. You'd never guess that being in the middle of 13 children there'd be an introvert in the crowd. I was. Still am. People think because I am a passionate and eloquent orator, that automatically defines me as extroverted, outgoing, life of the party. I can be all of that. My preference? Being here in this space, with the family who asks nothing of me but to place my trash in the appropriate receptacles so they won't be drowned by it or even worse, if there is a worse, poisoned. My preference is to be with someone who understands me and thinks I'm terrific anyway. I enjoy gatherings in doses. Crowds when necessary. Even then, I'd prefer to be seen and not heard so much. Perhaps I am an extrovert who was disciplined, cajoled, manipulated, and intimidated into being an introvert.

I sit sometimes and attempt to conjure up my childhood. First grade. Parents coming for field days and special events. I just can't. I know. There are many reasons they could not come to my activities. I don't even want to think about them. After all, they're only excuses. I worked also. I had other obligations also. I got tired also. I was frustrated sometimes also. I can't remember a graduation, school play, chorus event; I was co-chair of the Ft. Barnwell High School Bulldog's Cheerleading Squad two years, football and basketball. I can't recall a time either of my parents came to support me. Even now I want to spare them (may they rest in peace) and say perhaps they did. No. They didn't.

"Where's that money I gave you to put up for your momma girl?", my dad would ask as he sat on the edge of the bed, swaying drunkenly. "I gave it to her already," I replied, with the sincerity of a 10 year old. "No, you didn't. She hasn't even been home yet," came his breathy retort. 'Yes, she did, Ben," I said. [Interestingly enough, we always called our dad by his first name.] "She came home and I gave it to her and then she left." I had to stick to my story because my mother said when Dad gave me the money for her I was not to tell him where I put it or we wouldn't have food for the next week. "Get your scrawny ass over here girl, and you better tell me where that money is, cause you are telling a damn lie." My dad was growing angrier every second. I tried to back out of the room where he sat, but couldn't. He was my dad. I had to stay there, keep lying, hoping my mom would return any minute. Sometimes she did, and I could run under the porch or to one of my abandoned cars.

There were times she took too long and I ended up giving my dad the money he had left for his family to live on during the next week. And for what? So he could drink it up down at the neighboring juke joint or one of the houses he frequented throughout the weekend. i was one of the lucky ones. Being the middle child, I was rarely the one he gave this hedge fund to, but when he did, I always lived in fear every second until he either came to take it back or my mom came to get it. Which doesn't mean he didn't come to take it back; it meant only that she had more experience about what to do than I did. The down side of that of course, if she did not give it back, a fight would ensue. She would get hit; he would call her very bad names, and sometimes after all of that, she would give him some of the money back.

Many times I hated my parents. Both of them. My dad for being a drunk and causing so much pain to my mom; my mom for staying there and allowing him to do it. The cops were at our house many a weekend. Seems it took them longer and longer to respond to the 911 calls. She'd always take him back. A couple of times she made him stay away longer than usual. But she always took him back. He'd cuss her out. Call her the most awful names.

There was one time my dad came home from one of his drunken bouts. And the argument began immediately. I was in the bedroom asleep when the commotion awakened me. My youngest three sisters were in the bed with me. My mom had been cooking, and she walked into the kitchen to check on her food. My stomach was in a terrible knot. I had sat up in bed. Every time they argued, which was all the time, my stomach would knot up and I'd sweat and shake, and wish my dad would go away and never ever come back to our house. But he always came back. And they kept arguing. This night, my mom had opened the oven to inspect the food. I don't know why he was so mad that evening. I remember walking by just at the moment he pushed her head into the damned oven! WITW! "Oh Lord, Ben ," my mother wailed! He just stood there as if she deserved what she got, a wry grin on his face. And then he saw me.

I ran to the back porch and got the broom. Came running into the kitchen where they were. 'Leave my momma alone!" I screamed, raising the broom frantically over my head, shaking to the core. I exploded with pent up anger and frustration. "If you touch her again, I'll hit you with this broom, Ben, I mean it!" And I meant it to, as I advanced towards him. My dad was over 6'; I was barely 4' at that time. None of that mattered to me. I felt like a volcano that had been lying dormant for ages and was about to spew volumes of ash and coal and death.

My mother spoke then. Gently. "Sweetie," she said, blood streaming from a cut on her lip and scratches to her face. "Put the broom down." "What? What did you say? I'll hit him with this broom, mother. I'll hit him to death with it." I repeated over and over as if I was on automatic pilot. I don't know when I had been so mad in my entire life. "No," she said, weariness creeping into her voice. Perhaps concern for me. "He's your daddy. And as long as you live you will need to respect your daddy."

What did she say to me? This fool had just shoved her head into an oven, after hitting her across the face, and she was protecting him! "If you say that to me, then maybe he should be beating you." I was livid. This was outrageous. I looked at my mom. In that moment, my mother seemed so worn. Broken. Old. Her spirit seemed shattered. And I looked at him "You'd better be glad she came to your rescue," he said, weaving and bobbing as he always did on weekends. "I was about to stomp the shit out of you." I was no longer afraid. I saw something in his eyes. Fear. Respect. Confusion. I was the runt of the litter and I had the gall to stand up to him, with a weapon no less. I walked out of the kitchen with confidence and poise, as if I dared him to make the slightest move towards me. I believe I would have fought that man in that kitchen. And I'm certain he knew it.

That day was a turning point for us, my dad and me. It was when I realized that I had an evil side to my sweet nature, and if pushed to the limit, it is possible that I could seriously hurt someone that I loved. I truly wanted to kill my dad that night. I felt it all over me. Perhaps this is why I could never fight the men with whom I was in a relationship. Fear kept me from it. I put the broom back on the porch. On a couple of occasions after that night, my dad said to me, "You're the only child I got that I let talk to me like you do." What was my response to that? I did not have one. I never did. I just looked him straight in his eyes with a crooked smile on my lips. There was nothing left to prove between us. He had shown me everything he was. And I had shown him my potential. The cycle was vicious. It did not stop. He'd beat her. She'd beat us. And it lasted for many, many, years. Sometimes even when there was "company" at our house.

When love is unreliable and you are a child, you assume that it is the nature of love—its quality—to be unreliable. Children do not find fault with their parents until later. In the beginning the love you get is the love that sets. — Jeanette Winterson

CHAPTER

17

One day my parents were in the back yard having a cookout. All of the children were playing outside. My uncles and aunts and their children were there. Things were going smoothly; one of the few times we were having fun as a family. "What the hell you mean by that?" My mom had responded to a joke my dad had told; he was furious. "By what? What are you talking about, Ben?" My mom queried. "That damn shit you just said. What the hell did you mean?" my dad continued as he crouched upon my mom in an attack mode. "You children go on inside and play somewhere," one of my aunts said. We shuffled as if to move, but were rooted to the spot. "I don't know what you're talking about," my mom said, a croak in her voice. 'You were telling jokes and I just told a joke. What are you all up in the air about?" she asked. "I'll show you what the hell I'm mad about," my dad stormed. Out of nowhere, he hit my mom on the side of her head with his fist. "Oh no, Ben," she said, as she jumped from the porch and began running down the back path from our house.

It seemed my dad literally flew after her. We started hollering, "Somebody get my dad, don't let him hit our mom. Uncle John, Uncle Calvin. Go get him!" They looked at us. Shushed us the best they could. Mumbled something about everything being alright. And waited for my parents to come back to the house. They did, of course, with my dad holding my mom as if he loved her with all his heart, and with her lip bleeding and her eye swollen, she held on to him for dear life. Let the good times roll! What a crock load of crap! I saw that and would wonder what kind of God is there that could watch a man beat a woman like that and do nothing to stop it. Ever! God was never very helpful when one needed God to be.

My dad could "out curse a sailor." Words that came from his mouth when he was angry were outright detestable. He'd call my mom all kinds of bitches, whores. He'd accuse her of men and sleeping around. He even told me once that I was just like my mother. This happened after I got pregnant with my son. A few hours after I came home from the hospital, my dad came home. Yes, intoxicated. "Where's that damn baby?" he asked my mom, who was preparing a bottle for Malek. "In there with his mom," she replied. He came to the room where my son and I were. I met him at the door. "Ben," I said, "let me bring him to you later. He just went to sleep and he's been cranky since we got home." Weaving towards the entrance even closer, my dad was not to be outdone. He came into the room, went to reach for my son. I would not let him pick up Malek. "Not now, Ben," I said. 'He is asleep and I'm tired. I'll let you know as soon as he wakes up."

It's not that I thought he'd use reason and just go on back to the room he shared with my mom. I was hoping that this once, he'd play nice and go away. With a vengeance that was uncharacteristic even for him, he replied, "You can take that goddam baby and your goddam self and go over to his dad's house and live if I can't touch him. Ain't no goddam body going to tell me I can't hold a baby in my own goddam house." My eyes teared up immediately. Hot. Scalding. I couldn't believe what I had heard. "It's not that you can't hold him, Ben," I tried to soothe him with my words. By now Malek was waking up anyhow. "It's just that he's asleep. He's going to wake up in a few minutes. And I just need to rest for awhile." "Goddam that. Take him on out of here, goddamit. You and the baby can go live with his mother fucking daddy."

With that, he teetered out of the room. Malek awoke of course. And I sat there, stunned, hurt, too weary to even think. I held my son and rocked him with all the love I could muster. Cried the biggest tears I had ever cried, I believe. And I promised my child that he and I would not live in this house very long. I would take him away from all the misery that comes with living at 1112 Magnolia Street. It took almost two years, but we moved away to his dad's house, who had become my husband by this time. True to his word, my dad did not warm up to his grandson until many years later. Not by his own choosing, I regret to say. Malek was such a gentle, sweet, loving little boy; it was just impossible not to love him.

The scary and absolute crazy thing about this story is that the man you're reading about now was not always a lousy person. He wasn't. Many times we'd sit around a pot of turtle stew he was cooking and sing some Sam Cooke or, my absolute favorite to hear him sing, Otis Redding's "Sitting on the Dock of the Bay." My dad loved that song and he could out croon Otis any time! He and I would sing it together. On occasion, he'd tell some very good jokes and we would laugh until our stomachs hurt. It was fun to go to Dudley with him and spend time with his mother, sisters and brothers, Aunt Elizabeth, Aunt Helen, Uncle John, Uncle Calvin, Uncle Sam, and all the cousins. And when Uncle Grant and Aunt Aretha came to visit with our cousins, Lucy and Janice, my dad was always a good sport. I think it had something to do with the fact that Uncle Grant was a preacher. Or maybe he simply had a closer relationship with that particular brother. I don't know.

Once we went to Nags Head, the whole family. My dad was installing the plumbing for some fancy hotel. That was a great time. He didn't share that side of himself with us often. Every now and then we'd see him and our mom holding hands and sitting very close together, sometimes she'd sit on his lap. These moments were few and far between. And they many times ended up ugly. They just did. There is one thing I can say with a certain degree of pride. No one messed around with Ben's children. No one.

My dad would get drunk on weekends. And he would act up bad at home and do all the things you just read and more. But he'd beat the hell out of anyone who screwed around with his children. And so, no one did. No one, of course, except him. Not so much physically-- I never recall being spanked by my dad. But psychologically and spiritually, the damage is so extensive to the point that many in my family would dispute the facts presented herein. My dad was an abusive man. And he was never the wiser.

Despite all of that, I loved my dad. He was, after all, my dad. I was supposed to love him. It was the teaching of the church. It was the teaching of society. And it most certainly was what my mother taught me to do. But I think it was more than that. I thought he was the most handsome man in the world, especially in the world I knew. He was tall. Slim. Muscular. Dark mustache and brows. His smile was oh so charming. I used to think he could charm the rattler from a venomous snake. And that voice—oh, he could sing! His voice was magical; my dad's melodious notes could rival any bird or wind chime. And he had such a beautiful, hearty laugh. The whole place would instantly light up when my dad was present and at his best.

When my dad was happy, not drinking, or cussing, and just my dad, I preferred being with him than any other person on the planet, even my mom. He was so funny. And charming. I remember the twinkle in his eye when he smiled, and the way his lips would curl up in the corner when he bellowed with laughter. I grew up in a place surrounded by segregation, labeling, dis-ease, hard work—tobacco fields, cucumber picking, cotton patches, blueberry farms, to name a few. Granted, I was the middle child so I got to dodge most of that kind of labor because the older siblings had to do that work while I stayed at home and looked after the younger ones.

I lived for those moments with my dad. Those joyful times. They were few and far between. Most of the time, my dad was an alien that I wished many nights would return to the planet for evil, mean, nasty men like him, that place far, far away. I recall the words of Jenna in the movie, Forest Gump. Jenna was hiding from her dad in the cornfield, and she began to pray: "Dear God, make me a bird, so I can fly, far, far away from here." She repeated it over and over. Needless to say, she did not become a bird, and her dad found her in that cornfield.

Perhaps I didn't always love my mother either. I saw her as weak. Whiny. Sniveling. Afraid. It was years later that I understood the strength my mother had. It wasn't until after I had been in my own relationships with my husbands (dad all over again) and my own children, that I realized my mother did the best she knew to do with the options she had been given. I know now just how strong she truly was. It is impossible to live under certain conditions even with prayer and faith, without strength, determination, and will power. I know that now because when people ask me how could you stay there, or what were you thinking when, or why don't you just… Well. Now I know.

One of the reasons I think I hated Ben so much was because I loved him so much and to think that he could treat my mother the way he did and the children also, it was just one of those things that made me want him to just go away and not come back. One day he did. Twenty years later. Of course, by then, I no longer felt the same. I did not want my dad to die. He went to the doctor one day, was hospitalized, and within three weeks, he was dead. Lung cancer. The pain of his death was excruciating.

I've never been one to do a lot of crying. At least not in public, not even among my sisters and brothers and family. I wouldn't be surprised at all if my family thought I didn't care that my dad had died, or that I was coldhearted. Many of my siblings were aware of the love hate relationship my dad and I shared. I wasn't coldhearted. Not even stubborn. My grief was my own to bear in the way I needed to do so. I remember sitting in the funeral service, wanting so badly for the tears to fall. Everyone around me was crying in earnest. I pinched myself to make tears well up in my eyes. They did, but only for a moment. Not long enough for others to see.

So. I just dabbed at my eyes and held my face in my hands like I'd seen people do countless times. I would have made a superb actress! Or lawyer! By the time my dad died, I had been hurt so much. I had cried so many tears in the privacy of my abode, car, walks along the river. Tears represented some kind of weakness for me. And, I've never witnessed any good they've actually done. Whatever the situation was before the tears continues to be the situation after your face is all contorted and red, eyes bulging out of your head, and mucus clogging your nose and running down the side of your lip. Why get all disfigured like that when it changes absolutely nothing! That's my thinking anyhow. Still, I wanted to cry, because tears were all I had left for the loss my dad's death had presented in my life. Yet, sitting in that sacred space, surrounded by mourners, family, flowers, presence of God, the midst of his death and funeral—the tears just wouldn't flow. I was quite disturbed with my inability to express my grief with tears.

I didn't forgive my dad until he was on his bed dying of lung cancer. By then, I had a second son, Austin. When I visited my dad in his hospital room, I placed that little three-month old bundle of love on the bed next to him. My dad reached for my son. Rubbed his face, and smoothed his hair. Ben's smile was so bright. And Austin seemed to offer him a warm smile in return. My son never even cried to be picked up by unknown hands or held by these unfamiliar strong arms. He looked with contentment into his grandfather's eyes and melted right into his heart. A feeling of complete peace and love flooded my whole being. And I reached out my arms to my dad, hugged him, and said 'I love you Ben." My dad and I knew in that moment we were as we were before the rift that had divided us, before I conceived my first son.

Faith is seeing light with your heart when all your
eyes see is darkness around you.

CHAPTER 18

I wish I could say that all was well in my life from that moment forward and I had a better understanding of men and how to choose the right man for my life. Not so. My dad's accusations and name calling followed me throughout my life as I began to build relationships with other men, and with friends. The man I had loved and married in the early years of my adult life, and the man I had loved and married and with whom I had given birth to the son my dad held on his hospital bed were not the best choices for me.

They were wonderful human beings, God fearing, one of them was at least hardworking, but they both abused me, in one way or the other. And I stayed with them much longer than I should have once the abuse was recognized, because I believed with my whole heart that it was my Christian duty as a wife and mother to do so. It is what my mother did. And her mother before her. And I'm sure her mother before her. It's what mothers for generations in our family have done. This kind of curse is the theme of an upcoming book: *The Fourth Generation—Curse of the Libido*!

I was taught to believe that God (Jesus actually) was going to fix it for me. Well, if Jesus "fixed" it, it was through divorce (could this have been Jesus) and death (God forbid), with a whole bunch of hell in the between times, not just for me, but our children and my husbands. One of my husband's was almost killed by one of our children. Is that Jesus fixing it? Oh my word, no! Jesus didn't fix it for my mother either, unless you want to say that after over 45 years of that kind of abusive love, my dad got lung cancer and died, leaving my mother a little less than four years to enjoy some kind of freedom and happiness from his torture until her own demise. Of course God is known to take a long time making wrongs right in people's lives. The Israelites were enslaved over 400 years before God decided to send a deliverer, and God certainly knew all the abuse and evil that was being perpetuated on them. I have very little tolerance for that kind of self righteous theology or that kind of abusive god. It is what it is.

I tell Natalia, Austin, and Aubrey all the time that love is not supposed to devalue, demonize, or demoralize a person. And I caution them to get the hell out of abusive relationships—regardless of the kind of abuse. "But Mom, what if you truly love the person?" one of my children asked me. 'You don't," I respond. "You love the idea of what the relationship could be if...," I tell them. God does NOT want you in that place. I'll go to my grave preaching that. If you are not living an abundant life (which is what following the teachings of Jesus really will give us), then pack up your stuff and get the hell out of dodge. There is no man or woman anywhere under the sun worth torturing yourself and suffering abuse for. Not a one. I don't care how good the sex is. Economic status. Education. Nor how often you hear her or him say Praise the Lord. Run! Take it from one who knows, you can find some good suff from someone who knows how to treat you like the wonderful daughter or son of the Creator of the Universe that you are.

And can I say this? I will! If you can't find him or her, try Adam and Eve© until God shows you where Janetta or Steve is. And preachers, don't clog up my blog with scriptures about how touching your own body and loving your own self is a sin. If you do, you are more screwed up than you even know. Has anyone ever wondered what those men did on those moonlit, starry nights when they were in the wilderness, or on the boat naked (read your Bible), or on the mountaintop. Or were there no vaginas or penises in the first century? Oh well, then. Go ahead and close the book now if your purified eyes and sanctified minds can't deal with reality. Why are we Christians so hell bent on being ignorant and homophobic about sexuality when the whole world is filled with sex? Oh my word! Come out of the closet already!

I don't know what age the disciples were, but Jesus lived to be only 33 (depending on what gospel you're reading) and I have him beat by close to 25 years. I know what my body goes through in this house all alone. And, no, it's not a hot flash either! If the church was bold enough to speak truth, to the prophetic voice on the edge, these are the kinds of things that would prevent a lot of perverted, distorted, dysfunctional people walking around all schizophrenic from attempting to be holy and righteous on Sunday and hot as the noon day sun on Saturday nights! As if they are not one and the same.

Is it possible that right teaching could have prevented me from rushing to the altar the second time around for fear that I would go to "hell," eternal damnation because God created me with a very workable vagina! Staying in abusive relationships because I didn't want to end up never having sex again! Who wants that, for heaven's sake! The most beautiful part of creation is this ultimate expression of two people (well, I have to admit to my limits here) sharing the spiritual, emotional, psychological, and physical joy in connecting as one together (I'm not talking about marriage) in love and joy to the other. And yes, I have to admit to my own limitations again, but commitment, not just hopping in and out of beds across the coast because there are so many beautiful bodies out there. There are. And that's my bias. But. Alas. I'll hold on to that one.

In many ways, both my husbands were replications of my dad. I don't know what I expected from men. I just know that, from what I learned as a child growing up in a little town called Fort Barnwell, they never disappointed me. It is obvious that my staying with them met their expectations also. But no more. My pastor from a little country church in Pineville, preached a sermon one night he called: "Don't Go Back into Egypt." Read the story. Through Moses's leadership, God delivered the Israelites from bondage out of Egypt and they began to complain and moan and blame him at the first indication of a little inconvenience. One of the things they said to him was "we should have stayed in Egypt. At least we could have buried our dead!" For real. You had been whipped. Beaten. Maimed. Your male sons killed at birth. Your women raped. And you want to go back to Egypt for more of the same just so you can bury the dead. Please! You better get to cremating some folk.

I have applied that sermon to my life since the night Rev. Kirkwood, pastor of my home church, preached it during a revival. Most of the time, I've been able to live that life. Only now, twenty years later, am I on the path to applying it to my relationships with the men in my life. I refuse to go back to the kinds of relationships I've experienced with men and stay stuck in them for anyone, even Jesus. I know better than that now. First of all, Jesus would never want that from me. Never. And God does not want that for you either.

I confess my experiences have not been great. My faith gives me hope that there is light at the end of the tunnel. I still bring some of my baggage with me from my early years, what I observed and lived. The difference is, in most cases, I'm able now to move on when I am convinced that any relationship, whether one about love, friendship, leadership, no matter what, if the relationship invalidates me as a princess of God, a true daughter of the Creator of the Universe, and one whom God favors, I'll move on. It is still challenging for me not to invest my heart in a new relationship. I still hope to hear the words of love and devotion. In Tyler Perry's, *Family Reunion©*, Frank, who is the groom said to his bride: "*When I look at you I know that there is a God and that God loved me so much that God created you.*" I've not heard such or similar words. Why not me? I live for the day that God will grant me this kind of love. It sounds like the Apostle Paul's meaning in the Roman epistle when he writes about "unconditional love". The kind of love God has for me. I want that in my life. I'm determined not to settle for anything less than that going forth. God promises that if I make my delight in God, She will give me the desires of my heart.

These thoughts and more played footsies with my mind as I watched my dad hold my son. My dad died that day, after holding Austin and introducing himself with a heart filled with love. That is the legacy I had hoped to pass on to them, Austin and Aubrey (whom my dad never met), and my first children, Malek and Natalia. When he died, a well of knowledge and wisdom died with him, all of which I needed in order to break free of the chains that were holding me hostage in life, most especially love. I realized that day I had much left to learn. I could never be free until I came to terms with the reality of my early years, those formative years they have been called. I could not leave a legacy of strength and integrity for my children, until I first discovered who I am, which I believe begins with my discovering who God is.

The day I met you my life changed. The way you make me feel is hard to explain. You make me smile in a special kind of way. You make me fall deeper in love every day. — Unknown

CHAPTER 19

I'm in a new relationship now. His name is Nathanael. We went out for the first time eight months after his initial telephone contact. To this day, I cannot think how he came to have my number. We began talking late into the night about any number of things, from the beautiful full moon to the role of faith and church in our lives. Granted, I had been warned to stay away from him. The rumor mill had him pegged as a womanizer, but what single, accomplished, handsome man has not held that title by others?

I was not oblivious to the remarks and rumors of the natives in Jackson County. After all, I am quite new to it. When Nathanael began calling me, I told him right away I would not be interested in anyone who only wanted a casual fling. I had no desire to be a notch on his or anyone's belt. His response: "Get to know me for yourself."

After a few months of regular phone calls, I asked Nathanael if he was asking me out on a date. "I'll not ask you out until I'm sure you will say 'yes'", he responded. "I couldn't stand it if you turned me down." He said he couldn't stand it if he asked me out and I said no. That was way sweet, I thought. Yes. I was about to be hooked. We went around and around like that for a few months, flirting, teasing, discovering. "Do you see that lovely moon out?", he asked one night. "No, I haven't. I'm inside reading," I responded. "Take a moment. Go outside and look at it. It is beautiful." I'd go out on my back porch in Clyde while he was outside his house in Waynesville, and we'd look at the moon and talk about dreams and life and the beauty of the night. I prayed so much during this time. Earlier in the year, I had been let down by one person from this County and was determined not to get involved again with anyone else. My prayer: "God, give me the strength I need to avoid relationships and men who do not mean me any good. Don't let another man knock on my door and ask me out if he is not the right man for me." Nathanael and I had a serious bantering thing going on. I don't know if our attraction was so much physical at first, as least not for me, or more the chemistry that comes from two intellects meeting and finding compatibility and challenge in verbal discourse. Whatever it was, it grew.

Six months after we began our telephone talks, Samuel, my brother-in-law, died. I drove the 340 miles to be with my sister, Jennifer, during this time. Nathanael and I talked several times each day. The night I returned, I went immediately to bed. The next day, I was lethargic; I had stayed in bed all day. Maybe the magnitude of all I had been through was taking its toll. I had been unable to grieve during the process because my sister needed me. Sam's death and funeral occurred just one year six months after William's. Whatever the reason, I simply had no desire to move. When Nathanael called me that night, I was exhausted.

"Hey, what you doing?"

"Nothing. Just lying around'"

"I'm just leaving the gym. Going to get some food. Haven't eaten yet."

"Well, you're going to bring me some?"

"Sure I will. What do you want?"

"I don't know. Haven't been up all day. Exhausted and hungry."

"What do you like to eat?"

"My favorite is seafood. I'm somewhat easy when it comes to food."

"I'll tell you what. Just go ahead and rest. I'll get something and I'll be right over."

"You will? I look a sight. Have not been up all day."

"I don't care anything about that. I'll call you when I'm on the way."

True to his word, Nathanael arrived within 50 minutes. The aroma was wonderful. I was pale. He never missed a beat. "Where's the kitchen?" he asked. I showed him. "Ok. Why don't you sit down here? I'll get the plates and everything." "I don't mind helping," I began. "No. Let me do this for you, ok," he said, as he began to open cabinet doors, taking down plates, glasses, and utensils. I sat down in the well proportioned dining area. While he prepared the meal, I observed with renewed interest the beautiful painting of the Eucharist displayed on the bright, cream dining room wall. "Nathanael," I called out. "How do you like this rendition of the Lord's Supper." Nathanael brought the food to the table, along with the plates, glasses, and utensils. He admired the painting as he continued preparing the table for two. "Was that a gift?" he asked. It was. My best friends, Lisa and Alice had given it to me when I was ordained in Raleigh eleven years earlier.

When everything was ready, Nathanael poured a glass of wine for both of us, then reaching for my hand, clasped it in his own and blessed our meal. Then prepared both our plates. I will always remember our first meal, not only because of the menu, more because Nathanael had been so gracious and sweet to take care of everything. Shrimp cacciatore. Salad. Garlic bread. Pasta. I was overwhelmed. Nathanel would not permit me to get up for anything, preferring to cater to my needs. As hungry as I had been, I could only consume a small portion of the scrumptious dinner. At the end of the meal, Nathanael washed the dishes. He placed the leftovers in the refrigerator. "For later on," he said.

As he walked to the door to say goodnight, he touched my hand. "Can I get a sweet-sweet?" he asked. I smiled. "I have no sweet-sweet for you." With a huge smile, he hugged me slightly, opened the door, and left. Called me when he got in his car and talked until he was home. That was the beginning. I thought that to be treated like that was so unexpected and wonderful that I knew I would go out with him someday. That day would come barely two months later, and it would begin a whirlwind of romance between us.

I was not disappointed. From the outset, Nathanael met all my expectations and hopes in a relationship. We were amazingly compatible. I truly believed my prayers had been answered. One time he had said to me: "no matter what, don't change who you are to try to accommodate me. That would turn me off." I was not looking for a husband. Nathanael was not hoping for a wife. My desire was to be in a committed relationship with one man, who was content to be with one woman. I spoke this desire to Nathanael early in our relationship. We were on an outing in the Great Smokies of North Carolina.

"I am so thankful to God for meeting you Nathanael, and for being here with you," I said. "Leave God out of this," he responded. I turned to him, happiness ebbing from my heart. "How dare you suggest that I must leave God out of this! God is in everything I do, Nathanael, everything. And God is in this. If you think what we are to each other, or what we are doing is not honored by God, then let's pack up and take me back home right now." I was vehement. "You need to understand that if I believed in any way that God was not pleased with our being together, I would not be here. And I will thank God for everything and anything. All that I am is about who God is in my life. I am not ashamed to love you." He gave me a long, intense look. No other words were exchanged. He then came to me, touched my shoulder, and said "Ok. Ok." We've never had to keep God out of our conversations from that day forward.

Nathanael told me early on that relationships were challenging for him, and to allow himself to give his heart to another was almost impossible. It's not that I didn't believe him. I did. The more time we spent together, all indicators pointed to something very different. "The man I was at 40 is not the man I am today," he said. I began to feel that he had decided being with me was worth letting down his guard. And it was. For months. No one had ever held me as Nathanael did. I felt completely loved, valued, protected. Another time he said, "I asked myself, can this relationship get any better?" "Can it?" I asked. He said, "Yes." "How?" I asked. "Just continue doing what you are doing."

I did. We did. Scrabble. Cooking together. Watching dvd's at my house. Walks in the park. Picnics. Going for rides. Meeting at night just to rub noses. Long talks into the night. Roses. Waterfalls and wine. Jazz. Soul. Prayers. Sharing. "I'm about to hurt someone tonight. They did wrong by me." Nathanael's voice was alarming. An emotion I was not accustomed to was in his voice. "Think about it real hard, baby," I responded. "Ask yourself if it will be worth it in the end. You have a family who loves you and depends on you. I don't want anything to happen to you either." Our relationship was meaningful to both of us. Laughter. Sermon preparation. Secrets. Advice in business and pleasure. Nathanael and I shared so much.

Once we took a small day trip to a little town east of Clyde, where I lived, called Haywood. As we were sightseeing, Nathanael pointed to a cute little house that was for sale. "Let's buy that house", he said. I looked at him. My heart smiled so large. I chose not to respond, however, sensing that Nathanael was speaking out of character in the euphoria of the moment. "I've always wanted to live away from North Carolina in my next life," I said. "What are some places you would like to live if you were to move away?" I asked.

On the way back, he serenaded me, singing along with Barry White, "I've Got so Much to Give to You My Dear". I cuddled next to him in the front seat of the car, as much as I could with seatbelts, and rubbed the hair on his arm with my fingers and cheek. I enjoyed doing that. It was the happiest I had been in twenty years. I was certain that Nathanael was happy also. He would sleep so soundly, peacefully, in my arms. If I moved away, he would awaken and draw me close to him. "Where are you going?" he would say." I want to hold you." His kisses were the most gentle I had ever experienced. His bottom lip was so very sweet. I would often tell him that he is the most wonderful man I have ever loved.

Nathanael and I shared most things. He even told me that there was this woman he had known for years; they had grown up together he said. "If you ask me if I'm seeing other women. Yes. I see her from time to time. It's a dinner or something like that. I might go over to her house. There is no sexual intimacy between us. She's a good friend. There is no one I'm seeing in the way we are together. I'm not sexually intimate with anyone else." I did not know how to respond to that."Why would you tell me that?" I asked. I certainly didn't want him to go out with anyone, no matter how platonic the relationship might be. "You asked me," he said. "I just want to be truthful with you. One thing you can count on from me, even if it's not what you want to hear, is the truth."

We shared concerns about his place of business; my church life, other clergy contacts. Many times we shared disappointments, hopes, dreams with each other. We would laugh at things that happened in the community. Or even television shows. "Turn to channel 22 and let's watch The Waltons," he'd say. And we would sit in our different residences watching television together. He'd keep me abreast of the news on every level—local, state, national. "You need to stay on top of the news, darling," he'd say. "You're a pastor." "What is 'Abuela' doing tonight?" he'd inquire, after I'd told him that my granddaughter was spending time with me.

We talked about our children, how proud we were of them, and how they could be exasperating also. We talked about sex, and that had the potential to become pretty steamy sometimes! He often said that people used the word "love" too quickly and freely in relationships. We discussed marriage. Not getting married. That was not on either of our radar screens. Just marriage in general. I found it fascinating the time when he said, 'If I asked you to marry me, you'd say, come on let's go down to the beach and get married right now." Heart palpitations. Another comment to which I chose not to respond. Nathanael and I shared so much. Importance of communication. We talked about politics. Faith. Salvation. Heaven and hell. My thoughts were slightly more progressive than Nathanael's, but we never cancelled out the other.

At times when we were out to dinner, we'd observe the people around us and tell stories about them. This was a lot of fun. And we would do outlandish things and look around to make sure someone was looking! I did this more than Nathanael. He was a bit conservative in public. Not so much in private. He would help me think through a difficult problem. I provided him with that same kind of resource. We debated things the same way we loved; with heat and passion. Very little was orthodox between us. We were keen intellectuals. The competition between us was healthy and valued.

This is not a goodbye, my darling, this is a thank you.

— Nicholas Sparks

CHAPTER 20

Early in our relationship, Nathanael was questioning his own salvation, whether he was a true Christian. He had made some bad choices over the course of his life. It was as if he didn't believe God could forgive him for those choices. I spent a good amount of time encouraging him, assuring him that God has forgiven him and that he now has to forgive himself. "You are a good man, Nathanael," I would say. "You deserve to be happy, also, Nathanael, to love and be loved. Give yourself a break. Remember, God is concerned about your future, as in Jeremiah 39:11, a future with hope."

It was as if Nathanael was imprisoned in his mind in thinking that peoples opinions and judgments held power over him, "Let God love you, Darling Man!" I'd say to him. Many times, I would text him about the wonderful man he is, and the gift he is in my life. Nathanael never said that he felt those things. He would commend another brother or sister as if their relationship with God was on a higher level than his own. "Billy is such a righteous man. He doesn't smoke or drink, and he's still married to Sally, over 35 years now", he'd say, as if somehow Billy was righteous in ways Nathanael could never be. "I'm nothing like him. I mean, he does everything right." These statements would come up often between us. As of this writing, they've been few and far between. I feel good about being instrumental in some of his transformation of thought. "God knows your heart, Nathanael," I would say. "God knows that you are a man after God's own heart." After about a year, he began saying those things about himself. My heart smiled. An emotional connection had been made between us. We were bonding.

Then began the roller coaster relationship. "This County is not ready for us, Melanie. We can't continue on like this. I want to go out. We can't. We have to keep our relationship between us, private. Don't you want to go to lunch right here with someone sometimes? Go to the movies? We can't do that." Other times he would say: "I could not stand the thought that our relationship would be detrimental to your happiness in any way. I know that the people here would not want us to be together. You don't want me to say it, but it's true. Being with me is not good for you." How was I to respond to those things? I knew intellectually that he spoke wisely. Somewhat. I also knew what my prayers were.

Soon, however, I began to wonder if this was just a cover up for Nathanael to do what he wanted under the guise of protecting us from abuse of the people in Jackson County. Funny thing, I didn't have the courage to ask him that. Several times I almost did. Fear kept me from doing so. Fear held me in bondage, that speaking my truth would push him away. That had been the experience of my past. Once again, I felt that I was beginning to repeat the pattern of my past experiences. The very thing Nathanael told me never to do was the thing I was doing now. "No matter what, don't change to try to satisfy me. I love you just the way you are," he had said. I knew from past experiences this was not true, however, even past experiences with him.

Once when I had spoken out about something, he had become withdrawn, saying that he needed to hear from God. Another time, I had told him how I felt about him, Nathanael had stayed away from me over six weeks. No. Once again. I felt I had to keep my true self to myself, or the man in my life would find a reason to walk away. I could not be Me, Melanie. I had to be what he wanted or there would be no 'us'. That I could not be the strong, independent, vocal woman I am. That hurt. With Nathanael, I believed I had finally met someone with enough self confidence and personal esteem he would not be threatened by me, and with whom I could be real in every way. It was not to be.

I began to fall into Nathanael's routine. He did the calling. He decided when we could see each other. How did I allow that to happen? I wanted to be respectful of the fact that Nathanael did not have the flexibility I had. At first this was just fine. After all, I was not available on the weekends and as a pastor, I was always on call. It seemed plausible that Nathanael take the lead in making plans for when we would be together.

In the beginning, he would find many ways to make this happen. When his children visited with their little friends, Nathanael would come over for maybe an hour or two, just to spend time with me. At night, sometimes after a very stressful day as CEO of his own firm, he would come over and share a meal; many times we prepared a meal together. He was very relaxed with me. I'd remove his shoes, and massage his neck and shoulders. And I would whip his fine behind in Scrabble every time! Sometimes we made a game of it. He always had to pay the piper. One day, he decided that these times were taking unnecessary risks, that "if we were discovered, I would be ruined. And so would he".

I felt powerless to change the tide. I had decided that to be with him on his schedule was better than not being with him at all. It wasn't his commitments, obligations, and responsibilities that began to concern me. It was the feeling that Nathanael would give up on us before giving our relationship a chance, that he would give in to peoples' opinions rather than trust God to have our backs.

I continued to believe that God would work out the kinks on our behalf, if we both wanted it. I believed that God had granted us favor, and that "if we put out trust in God, God would give us the desires of our heart." It was during one particularly painful roller coastal moment, I treated myself to breakfast at one of my favorite restaurants, Cracker Barrels. During my meal, I invited a man who was sitting alone across from me to join me at my table. I cannot explain exactly why I got enough courage to do this. It was completely new for me. As I sat at my table, feeling unattractive, unloved, undesired, just miserable, I decided to do something bold for a change. I had no expected outcome, except to validate that all the "uns" I was feeling were myths. Leaving the restaurant, I was more convinced than ever that I was a beautiful woman, worthy of notice and love. I also was aware that for most of my life I had determined my worth and value by my relationship with a man, and that the lens through which I measured my relationships were those of my parents.

In my honesty, and desire to mend the rift between us, I shared this incident with Nathanael. It didn't go over well. This man who had told me so freely that he was seeing another woman in a platonic relationship, didn't trust me to have breakfast with a complete stranger in a public place. The hypocrisy of his response was unbelievable. I understood his chagrin to know that I had 'picked up', his words, a complete stranger. "There are all kinds of sick people in the world," he had said. Even so, I was thoroughly miffed that Nathanael responded as if I had no right as an adult woman to share a meal with someone other than him. I knew my intentions. I had no interest in the man as a possible date. The man and I understood this. We were just two ships in that moment, passing at sea.

I also was baffled that when I voluntarily told Nathanael about the pickup and the reason for it, he chose to concentrate on the fact that I picked up a stranger rather than his behavior towards me that I felt drove me to invite the man to my table. "You sure do push the envelope", he said. Another time he said, "You are a piece of work; not a problem, but a piece of work, girl." I shared my hurts and fears with Nathanael in long texts that I would write late at night, when everything was quiet and I could think. I admit that some of my words were like thorns. "The drama is too much for me. It's as if you have me on a schedule that only you know about. When will it be my turn to see you again?" "I can't believe you said that," he said to me. "You're not on a schedule; you don't have a time when it's your turn." I could feel the dismay and hurt in his voice. Most of the time my words were so sweet: "Another lovely day. My heart smiles knowing that you are somewhere in my sphere, tall, handsome, wonderful..." This was our life together.

The roller coaster continued. My friends chided me for being played by him. I never believed that. They simply couldn't know. "I'm the one he holds. I'm the one he talks with. I'm the one he sings to. I'm the one he laughs with. I know it seems like that to them, but they aren't with him. I am." I am consoled with that. During his periods of absence, we'd find our way back to each other. I'd reach out. He'd relent. Things would be great for another few months. Then the cycle began again. 'I don't know what this is between us," he often said. 'I don't know why God has brought us together. We both know that what we have between us is bigger than just us."

Was I reading too much into his words? "It's my fault that we've gotten as close as we have. All the sharing and phone calls, going out. The more you do things together the closer two people become. It's my fault," he'd say. Sometimes late at night, he'd hold me and say, "You've been hurt enough. You deserve the best." My heart would melt when he talked like this. Once he had said to me, "I want to do something for you I've never done with any other woman." I waited with abated breath. He could be so brutally honest sometimes. I did not know what to expect. "I want to wash your feet." How super sweet is that? What an humbling visual, and a true act of love, for him, and for me.

The challenge is he is on the run. I believe with my whole heart that God indeed orchestrated our meeting, that because of God's favor, Nathanael and I share this sacred space together. I also know that I can't be the one to hold us together. It is too painful for me. Many nights I toss and turn, sometimes crying in my pillow. I feel my self esteem waning. "Where are you God! Where are you?" That has become my constant prayer. The reality of having one's love rejected is overwhelming. The cycle continues. A promising relationship threatens to destroy me. Am I destined to be, once again, clawing my way to health and wholeness, a phoenix, rising from the ashes of despair!

I can be changed by what happens to me. But I cannot be reduced by it.

— Maya Angelou

EPILOG

Here she sits, glorying in the beauty of the lake, the ducks lazing on its quiet and tranquil stream. She is at an impasse about whether the love she's feeling for the new man in her life will yield the same kind of harvest she has known in the past, or more abundance than she's ever known with a man. One thing is certain. Melanie thinks that Nathanael is a hell of a man. For real! She has been praying out of the wazoo about them. Ok. She knows she shouldn't be so carnal. She has been praying with her whole heart about him, the two of them.

Melanie refuses to be stuck in an abusive relationship with a man again. She believes she is able to move on if she feels that she is. It seems that she always puts up a good fight at first. Therein lies the rub. She does not want to fight anymore. She wants to be in a mutually loving and caring relationship. Is this the one? She does not know. Melanie recalled the Henry Wadsworth rhyme: "…when she was good, she was very, very good, but when she was bad, she was horrid." Nathanael has many attributes she wants in a man. But how can a woman love a man when the man gives you the best of himself then decides midstream that he does not want to give "that part of himself" away? How can the woman then be content with just a little bit of what was so very wonderful from the same man? Wadsworth was not talking about Melanie. The poem was about Nathanael. He was so wonderful to her when he chose to be. When he decided he was becoming too emotionally attached, he became lukewarm towards her. And that was horrid.

One thing Melanie has come to realize. "God cannot use a woman with relationship drama," she had heard a preacher say once. It resonated within her heart then. It still does. Melanie spends a lot of time thinking about her relationship with Nathanael. She does ministry. She works hard. She is a good preacher and teacher. She really gives her church and her parishioners her very best. The truth. There are times when her relationship has a direct bearing on the energy and passion she gives her church. It does. Not only that. She also finds that when she should be praying about matters at the church, she is thinking about or praying for her relationship with Nathanael.

Let's face it. Vessels of Clay United Church of Christ deserves better. She has many gifts. She does find herself giving her relationship more attention than her ministry, which is akin to idolatry. She knows this is not the path she should travel. "Seek first the kin-dom of God..the kin-dom of God is within you." Do not place anyone or anything before God, before yourself. You are important. Melanie admits that if her relationship was mutual, in every way, she would be able to give herself more fully to her church, and to God. She wants to share this discovery with Nathanael. Fear keeps her from it. He has said many times he does not want to be a hindrance to her in any way. "You love me enough to give up your church for me," he had said once during a long telephone conversation when they were talking about moving on. "You can't do that. I could never live with that." Melanie had not responded. As much as she loved him, she would not give up her church for their love. That was not the issue. She would give all she had to find a way to have both. She believes that God has given her both. If only Nathanael would stop fighting and see the beauty God had given them to share.

She admits to herself that, loving Nathanael as she does makes her question her ability to see this relationship for what it is, move on, and wait for another. It causes her to ponder whether she has learned anything from her past experiences. At one point in her life, she contemplated therapy. She didn't think her Christian friends would understand her need for objective counseling. In her heart and head, she was convinced that this was the best route for her under the current circumstances. One of the first questions her therapist presented to her was: "When have you ever been enough?" Melanie could only look at Dr. Mac. Blank stare. When she could only produce the same blank stare when he asked: "Who comforted you as a child?" Melanie was convinced she had made the right decision. She had sat in Dr. Mac's office and cried for over an hour.

How did she get to this place? How did a little country girl from the caramel sand and black dirt of Ft. Barnwell, a small town in the hills of eastern North Carolina, end up four children later, single, one dead son, ordained pastor, twice divorced, psychologically abused, on a flight from Long Beach, California having spent the past six days with the United Church of Christ family participating in the 29th General Synod of that Church, voting on resolutions, singing, marching for immigration justice--arrive at this place in her life? How on earth did she get to this moment?

It was July 5th, one day after Independence Day. Melanie's heart was aching—once again. She was on her way home from Long Beach, California, to Jackson County, North Carolina, where lived the most wonderful man she had ever loved, and he had been unavailable to her for more than six weeks. "I don't want to fall in love with anyone," he said. "It's not you. You're wonderful. You deserve so much more than I can give. I just don't want to give that part of myself away."

Hot, scalding tears threaten to spill onto her cheeks and run down her neck. Nathanael had never seen her cry. One night when they were together, she had said something about being about to cry. "Don't do that," he had said. "Why?" she asked. "I do not like to see a woman cry. If you cry, I'll have to leave." Imagine that, she hiccuped into her heart. If he could see me now, I wonder what he would think. The broken lines on the highway mimic the brokenness of her life. Melanie's throat is searing, as it constricts in its attempt to stem the agony of another failed relationship that had the promises of something beautiful, great.

"You give so much of yourself away," he had said. "I care about you a lot. You know I do. It's time to move on. Jackson County is not ready for our love. I don't want to be tarred and feathered by these people. You don't know how it feels to be the object of hate and ridicule. I've seen it. Remember, I'm a son of Jackson County. I don't want that for you; and

I don't want it for me either. I couldn't take it if I knew I was to blame for any hurt that comes to you from these people. I'll never be good enough for you. Your church will never accept us. It's just time for us to move on." Melanie searched her heart for God's favor. She asked again and again: "God, how could this be the result of my prayer?" A strange choking sound emitted from deep within the abyss of her bowels. A sound so agonizing she had to listen again to make sure it was her own, this guttural, wrenching plea to all that is holy to help her. Stop this. Don't let this be so.

As he waited for her to speak, she could feel the resolve that had seeped through his voice. A plea for understanding. A desire to be friends. A need for her to accept the inevitability of their need to move on without hate, anger, or accusations. There was also a resolution of finality in his voice. Nathanael was on offensive. It was clear that he did not want to hear any defense or argument from her about the reasons they should not move on. For him, all the scenarios had played out in his mind. That was that. Cold. Warm. Convinced. Final. Resolute. An unpleasant tenor to his voice that Melanie found strange, though not foreign; this sound had been reserved for those who stood in his way, never for her. Now the controlled patience in his voice was directed towards her.

It also was a haunting sound, as if the words he was speaking were not real, even to him. He waited. She had to say something. What was there to say? She had prayed. She had trusted God. She had believed. Still believed. Melanie knew he was right in many ways. She did not want to face that reality. She believed, with God's help, they could work through this dilemma. His words were not surprising. They most certainly explained his silence of the past few weeks, particularly during her time in California. This conversation had been looming over them for almost two months. It was the elephant in the room. Once she had accused him of multiple personalities. "You remind me of someone with schizophrenia," she had said during one of their evenings together. "So loving and wonderful one day. Aloof the next." They had laughed that night. Déjà vu. Except this time, there was no humor.

Was this just another of Nathanael's split personality moments! An involuntary shudder ran down her spine. Melanie's instinct was flight.

Whatever. All that they'd shared. The long talks late into the night. Trips. Preparing meals together in her home. Their laughter. Picnic in the park. Praying together for their children and each other. Writing sermons together. Nights when they would hold each other so closely and tenderly. The joy in celebrating love and life together. Was it easy for Nathanael to give up all of their love? "Why would you say it's easy," he had asked her. "Because, easy or not, you are saying let's move on. You are ready to give up," she responded. How could he be? She still could hear his unique beautiful voice as he serenaded her so often. When he spoke, she could feel his breath on her skin, feel his touch. "It's time to move on," he had said. For real. It's time to move on from all of that? Her lips wanted to form those words. The pain in her throat would not let her speak.

Melanie had known this day was inevitable. Not today, surely. She was not ready. She needed more time. But is there ever a right time, a good time to move on? Perhaps. Rarely can the best time be discerned in the midst of the struggle. In the silence that followed, tears cascaded down Melanie's face like a beautiful waterfall into the Niagara River. There was no beauty in this fall. There was only hurt. Pain. Complete devastation. Driving down the highway, she tried to imagine a life without the man she loved. The more she tried, the more the tears streamed down her face, into her hair, forming a tributary under her chin, and a puddle onto her lap.

All the way home, she had a vivid recollection of the conversation. She recalled earlier words he had spoken, words that had never left her mind from the first moment he had spoken them, two months earlier. "I don't want you to be hurt by our love. And if you truly love me, you wouldn't want that for me either." More truthful words had never been uttered. Sometimes love is just not enough. Sometimes love means letting go.

Then as now Melanie knew that their time would either have to end or Nathanael would have to decide to bring their relationship out in the open. There didn't seem to be a chance that he would ever do that. This eventuality was extremely painful for Melanie. For there was one thing she knew for certain. Melanie knew that she and Nathanael could not be just friends. "I need to let you know that I can't just be your friend, Nathanael", she said, the words coming in gasps and gulps. She was working hard to keep the sound of crying from escaping into her voice. "Don't say that," he said. "It's true," she said. "You and I have been too much together for me to now be your friend." "I hope that in time you will change your mind," he responded.

As so often happened between them they did not move on. Two days after the decision, Melanie texted Nathanael to say she now understood his meaning and that she appreciated him for looking out for her welfare, protecting her reputation. Nathanael called Melanie later that same day. "Can I come over?" he asked. When he arrived, it was as if the conversation about moving on never happened. In her words: "He came to me in the night. And it was as I imagined. To be in his arms. To smell his scent. To touch and be touched by him. Love and be loved by him. He came to me in the night. And it was all I imagined. Happy."

Smiling into his chest, she reached up to touch Nathanael's face, as his wonderful embrace clasped her to his long, powerful yet gentle frame. "What are you going to do with me, Nathanael?" she asked. 'I don' know", he responded, holding her even closer, "get a tutor." In that moment, their joy was complete. "When we go away for a few days, I'm going to wash your feet," he said. So unexpected. Voluntarily. Once again, she felt the bond between them. Her heart smiled.

Melanie's story is not about sex. It's not about pleasure. It is most definitely not about sin. It is about a woman who knows that she has God's favor, and is not sure how to allow that favor to manifest in her life. It is about abuse and pain and hurt. It is a story about trust and abandonment. Love and rejection. Risk and sacrifice. Her story is about living her life and having her say, with no fear or shame of what others will think. It is a story about being vulnerable and taking risks. It's about self-worth, knowing who she is and walking in the fullness and truth of that knowledge. Finally, it is a story about love, loving others, yes, but more to the point, loving one's self.

There is much Melanie does not know. One thing she holds onto. She has been created by God, *imago Dei*, to love, laugh, play, create, live, soar. She will never again settle for anything less, nor will she tolerate abuse in the name of love or necessity. As she is learning in therapy, there is a little girl inside who is hungry, thirsty, and needy. She is searching for the love of her father and mother, the comfort of being cared for and nurtured by the adults in her childhood, and the joy of being valued and seen by the man in her life.

Until that little girl is fulfilled, Melanie will continue to struggle with doubt and uncertainty, needing to be validated by the men in her life in the way her mother was never validated by Melanie's dad. The little girl is searching for love in all the wrong places. It is up to Melanie, now, to reassure the child within that it is time to grow up and live the beautiful life that Melanie has created for her. Melanie must prove to the little girl inside that she will take care of her, hold her, love her, value her. The little girl needs to be assured that Melanie can indeed take care of her, without depending on anyone outside herself to do so.

Face it. Melanie is a complex creation. As Nathanael said, "she is a piece of work." For you to grasp a broader stroke of who Melanie is, I need to start from the beginning. You are invited to surf these unchartered waters and continue on this journey to discovery with Melanie, in my future book: *Loved or Forsaken - The First Twenty Years.*

In May Sarton's work, "Now I Become Myself", I am repeatedly drawn to the first few stanzas, four lines of which I'm sharing herein. Her work has inspired me to write a piece in response. *"Now I become myself. It's taken time, many years and places; I have been dissolved and shaken, worn other people's faces, … O, in this single hour I live all of myself and do not move. I, the pursued, who madly ran, stand still, stand still, and stop the sun!"*

ME© by Dian Griffin Jackson

This is such a delightful poem. It truly speaks to me.
My very soul is singing and dancing with sheer pleasure!
Do you know how long I've wanted to be me?
Me, with all my own foibles, gifts, idiosyncrasies, assets—
Me. A most succulent word. Delectable. Refreshing.
Like an abundant waterfall dashing over rocks and fallen trees.
Me. The all and the not yet.
Laughter bubbles up inside, spilling over into pure ecstasy.
Imagine. I've been searching for her.
Running from her.
Afraid of her.
Seduced by her.
Embarrassed by her.
Yet, never once did she go away.
She never gave up.
Whenever I paused to reach within her depths, she was there.
Whenever I needed reassurance, strength, courage—
She opened herself and engulfed my scarred frame.
Healing. Soothing. Sending forth.
Me. Awesome. Phenomenal.
What freedom!
To be so aware and sure of the abundance of me.
The journey is not over. Never will be.
For this moment, I am me.

And I will live fully into the me that has always been.
The me that is – me.
ME.

Melanie is on a quest to wholeness, searching for the illusive ME, a trip to freedom—her own and hopefully through her journey, yours. As she finds liberty and salvation, you will find your own place to soar above the lake to a future of hope and peace. And remember, God Favors Melanie! God Favors You! We are all like the Phoenix. Rising from the Ashes!

Sermon

"I Don't Look Like What I've Been Through!"

Text – Mark 10:35-45

Subject – I Don't Look Like What I've Been Through

³⁵ James and John, the two sons of Zebedee, *came up to Jesus, saying, "Teacher, we want you to do for us whatever we ask of you." ³⁶ And He said to them, "What do you want me to do for you?" ³⁷ They said to him, "Grant that we may sit, one on your right and one on your left, in Your glory." ³⁸ But Jesus said to them, "You do not know what you are asking. Are you able to drink the cup that I drink, or to be baptized with the baptism with which I am baptized?" ³⁹ They said to Him, "We are able." And Jesus said to them, "The cup that I drink you shall drink; and you shall be baptized with the baptism with which I am baptized. ⁴⁰ But to sit on my right or on my left, this is not mine to give; but it is for those for whom it has been prepared." ⁴¹ Hearing this, the ten began to feel indignant with James and John. ⁴² Calling them to himself, Jesus *said to them, "You know that those who are recognized as rulers of the Gentiles lord it over them; and their great men exercise authority over them. ⁴³ But it is not this way among you, but whoever wishes to become great among you shall be your servant; ⁴⁴ and whoever wishes to be first among you shall be slave of all. ⁴⁵ For even the Son of Man did not come to be served, but to serve, and to give his life a ransom for many."

Prayer: Eternal God, as I open my mouth to boldly proclaim the gospel of love and power, let your transformative words ignite a flame of hope and new possibilities in someone's life. In this hour, may these truths be rightly preached and heard. Let the words of my mouth and the meditations of our hearts be acceptable to you, for in you we find our salvation and strength. Amen.

I DON'T LOOK LIKE WHAT I'VE BEEN THROUGH!

Scholars alert us that the writer of the gospel of Mark is about immediacy – urgency – being in a hurry. Within these words, we find that Jesus and the disciples are on the move. There is work to do before Jesus is betrayed, arrested, tried, and crucified. In his haste to fulfill his purpose in the earth, Jesus moves quickly towards Jerusalem. We are told that Jesus' destiny is tied up there. His fate awaits him. Or perhaps we could say, his very reason for existing is tied up in his sense of urgency to get to Jerusalem. As he journeys with his most trusted followers, a situation begins brewing among them that is uncomfortable. As a matter of fact, jealousy, anger, envy, and mistrust develops among the ranks. We know from previous studies in this gospel, that the writer is not concerned about making us feel good. This writer causes DISCOMFORT every chance he gets.

If you hope to read a feel good message, you've come to the wrong periscope. If anyone wants to feel good and "get your praise" on by thinking about what a wonderful Christian you are and how you got Jesus and that's enough, well, maybe the gospel of Mark is not the one for you. This gospel writer's primary purpose is to upset you, to call your attention to an alternative way of living and being, to following AFTER Jesus, so much so that the decisions you make might cause you to lose your very life. After all, when Jesus says if you want to follow me, take up your cross and deny yourself, well, that's exactly what he means. This is not a feel good gospel-it is a gospel that challenges us; it causes us to wrestle with where we are in Christ and says to us, change it, fix it, learn it, study it, do it—not my will but your will O God. If one can be complacent after sitting down with Mark, there's a problem. There are some people who, like the disciples, want the glory with no guts.

In this text, Jesus has given his final and most detailed prediction of what the future holds for him: trial, suffering, death, and resurrection. Now, he is about to enter Jerusalem for he has an appointment with destiny, to confront the temple-based aristocracy, you know, those who will keep some out and allow the privileged to come in. Those who sit in their comfortable positions of power and enforce traditions and rules on any who would come into God's house or live as children of God, though not adhering to those same rules for themselves. Here we have James and John, who appear to have missed everything Jesus has been teaching the disciples and the people about how to live as kindom people. What they had not missed, however, was that Jesus was somebody. Jesus was the Messiah. Jesus was the one, in their minds, who would overthrow the Roman political power structure and establish a new order and rule in Jerusalem. After all, they were right there during the transfiguration on the mountaintop; they knew Jesus was destined for glory. And they wanted to be in the center of power. These two mighty men of valor, the sons of Zebedee, believed that the authority that Jesus possessed would lead to something big, perhaps he would even become the next Ceasar, Emperor of Rome, who knows, maybe even King, and James and John did not want to miss out on their chance to ride into glory on Jesus' dime.

As we continue reading it becomes evident that the other disciples were of the same mindset. They were simply annoyed that James and John got to Jesus first. The other disciples are chagrined that James and John seek to outflank them in prominence, and Jesus has to correct all of them. He holds up the conventions of gentile (Roman) sociopolitical authorities as negative examples of the meaning of power in the kin-dom of God. He says to them that self-interest and self-protection cannot be permitted to trump justice in God's kin-dom. In other words, life in the kin-dom of God is not about obtaining power that one can lord over another. It's about being a servant, in the words of the prophet-poet Isaiah, a willing vessel used by God to "preach and live good news to the oppressed, an instrument empowered by the Spirit to bring good news to the poor, comfort the brokenhearted, proclaim release to the captives, set the prisoners free, to tell those who mourn that the time of the Lord's favor has come". You got it all twisted, James and John, power in the kin-dom of God is being about God's business. And the only way to have that kind of power is to go through some things.

Listen, now, to Jesus' words to the disciples: "Can you drink of the cup I will drink? Can you endure the baptism in which I'm about to be baptized?" In other words, brothers, you're looking at me and remembering my glory but I want you to know there is a story behind my glory. I have to go through the fire before I receive the glory. You've been with me for about two years and you know some of what I've had to endure. I don't look like what I've been through or what lies ahead for me. A cross awaits me. Nails await me. Torture awaits me. Abuse awaits me. Betrayal awaits me. Loss awaits me. My friends will walk away one by one. The time will come when I will feel that even my God has forgotten about me. Condemnation awaits me. They will hang me up and strip me of my dignity and my honor. They will call themselves dishonoring my God and my calling by nailing a (derogatory) name on the cross they nail me to, and by placing a crown of thorns on my head.

But don't worry about that, God is going to work in my favor in that situation. Jesus admonishes his followers to be wary of the glory, for with the glory, comes pain, anguish, abuse. He goes on to say, and I paraphrase, I'm not worried about any of that, for on the third day I will rise again. They will look for me in the tomb, where they thought they had cast me down and destroyed me. Oh, but God! I like this part, church. Say with me as you read this word, "but God"! God stepped into history, touched my body, spoke like into my dead situation, and said rise up my son. It's time for you to live! It's time for you to get up! They sealed the tomb. They wanted to destroy you. They wanted you dead. Oh, but Jesus said: I will rise again. I will rise again. And when I get up, the glory and anointing of God will be so powerful folk won't even recognize me. I'll look different. I'll look new. I'll look as if I've been on the mountaintop. The enemy meant to kill me. The enemy thought I had been counted out! But I need to tell someone today, the grave is just the place God used to prepare me for the great things in my life. I don't look like what I've been through!

I say to you, don't look at Melanie and say "I want to be like Melanie. Or I want to be like Jesus, let me be just like Rev. Jackson, or T.D. Jakes, or Joyce Meyer, Joel Osten—Jesus is saying, "Are you willing and ready to go through some hard trials for the sake of the gospel? Will you have the faith to hold out until the end? Will you be able to endure when folk talk about you, turn their heads and walk away? What will you do when your husbands don't appreciate you, when they treat you as less than a woman of God? Will you be willing to stand for the right when church leaders put you out of the church, won't let you preach in their pulpits, sing on their choirs, serve communion because of your gender and sexuality. Will you be able to trust me, stand on my promises, hold onto your faith even in the midst of the possibility of death? Church, right now I can hear someone saying, like Jesus, "I don't look like what I've been through."

Look at Jesus' witness. He's not known to focus on himself. This time he feels a need to share with his followers on a more personal, intimate way. Don't get it twisted, he says. I've been through some things. My own family and friends tried to kill me in my own hometown. They put me out of the synagogue. The church leaders have attempted to run me out of Jerusalem and the surrounding villages from the moment I began preaching and teaching and healing. I've had to rebuke one of my closest friends because he didn't understand God's calling on my life. Sometimes I've had to stay awake all night long. Many times I've had to minister to God's people with very little sleep. I've been hungry. There was a time the enemy tempted me in my weakest moment and I had to decide whether I'd follow God and a future with hope or give up everything for immediate fame and a piece of bread to eat, but I chose to obey God.

Jesus is saying to the disciples and to us today, oh, I've been through some things. I just don't look like what I've been through. I don't look stressed and beat down because God has been good to me. God has been there all the time. God's favor is on me. God has never given up on me. God has kept me in the midst of it all. And look. I will rise again, on the third day. And my closest friends won't even recognize me. They will expect grave clothes, bad breath, and unkempt hair. I will rise with all power in my hands—power to live and praise and glorify the God in me! I'm going to look good!

I leave this thought with you. What's your third day? Whatever you're going through, hold onto God. Your third day might be a month from today, a year later, but hold onto God's unchanging hand. Jesus went through hell's fire (not literally) for you and for me, but oh, just look at God, look how God worked things out in Jesus' life—high and lifted up, every knee will bow and every tongue will confess that he is Lord. He has been given a name above all names. He sits now with the Holy Spirit, God Triune—Creator, Redeemer, Sustainer. Hold on to your faith. Never give up on the God in you, for God never gives up on you. Believe in yourself, and you will rise – AGAIN!

Some things have to die in us. We have to be willing to be talked about and scandalized for the sake of the gospel of Jesus Christ. God is calling us to be that church that will open our doors to everyone, the church that accepts all those whom God sends to us, to love those whom others would hate, to welcome those whom others would turn away, to be a voice and an advocate for the poor and those on the margins of society. God is calling us to be the church that tomorrow requires and now is the time for us to answer the call. It might mean we have to lose some friends and family before God can give us increase. It might mean having to change our attitudes and being open to new ideas and new ways of being, but I hear our still speaking God saying to each of us: trust God—with all that we, and see won't God be glorified in us!

Open your hearts. Open your ears. Open your minds. Open your hands. Allow God to move on the altars of your hearts and get on board with what God is doing right now in your midst. God says to the prophet, "behold I am doing a new thing, can you not perceive it, I am making all things new". You see church, God has to allow us to go through some pruning. God has to shape us, and melt us, and mold us before God can do all God has planned for us. God promises that eyes have not seen nor have ears heard nor has it entered into the minds of humanity all God has in store for us. We will go through winter, spring, summer and fall, but in the end we will not look like what we've been through. God will be glorified in our church, in our families, our communities, and in each of us.

God was and continues to be glorified in Melanie's life. No. She didn't always get it right. She had some hard struggles in life. Her love was abused and misused. Sometimes she had to cry all night long. Can I take my time and preach for a minute, somebody? Melanie searched for love in all the wrong places. The little girl within her had searched for love and acceptance all Melanie's life. She loved and gave unconditionally of herself to Grainger, William and now Nathanael. She was cast down in all three relationships, but each time she got up. How did she get up? Just like Jesus in the grave, God touched Melanie on the third day of her pain, third day of her struggles, third day of her confusion, third day of her discontent, third day of her disenfranchisement. God reached within Melanie's bosom and said, "daughter, get up. It's not over. I see you. I'm with you. Rise up and walk. Get up, take up your mat and walk. And lo, I will be with you through it all." Melanie listened to her Inner Teacher, the inner Wisdom, we call her Spirit. Melanie's Inner Conductor said it's not time to give up. Stay on the train. Stay focused. Keep your eyes on the God in you, for greater is the One in you than all of your struggles, all of your enemies, all of your abusive relationships, all of your pain. God favors you, Melanie.

Melanie reached deep in the abyss of despair and found that even though the enemy of life had knocked her down and was standing over her for the count, God said, grab the rope. Pull on the rope, my daughter. Rope of faith. Rope of hope. Rope of love. Rope of forgiveness. Rope of peace. Grab the rope daughter and pull, and see if I won't do what I promised I'd do. Melanie struggled all her life. Looking for favor. Wanting favor. Desiring favor. And she found out that through it all, even when she thought God had forgotten all about her, God was there all the time. She was cast down, but God refused to let her be destroyed. In the name of Jesus, in every circumstance, Melanie was able to rise up and walk. But God! God was faithful in Melanie's life, through it all. Each of you reading this message, begin to say right now, no matter what you're going through or regardless of what you've been through, say with me: "I thank God because I don't look like what I've been through!" God favors me!

I DON'T LOOK LIKE WHAT I'VE BEEN THROUGH!
AMEN!

ABOUT THE AUTHOR

Dian Griffin Jackson is the sixth of 13 children, born in the coldest month of the year to William Earl and Nettie Mae Rogers Griffin. As a little girl, growing up in Grifton, North Carolina, she dreamed of being a wife, mother of six, lawyer, author, singer, preacher, and in *Who's Who Among.* She has earned two degrees, B.A., Sociology, North Carolina Central University, Master of Divinity, Duke University School of Theology, both in Durham, North Carolina. She is now completing the paper for her Doctor of Ministry at Hood Theological Seminary, Salisbury, North Carolina. Dian has been an ordained minister in the United Church of Christ for 13 years.

A passionate and enthusiastic advocate for justice and truth, Dian resides in the sandhills of North Carolina, in a small town called Rockingham, where she serves as Senior Minister of Mt. Zion United Church of Christ, 986 Ledbetter Road, Rockingham. There she speaks truth to power, questioning traditional hermeneutical interpretations of Scripture, and standing on the wall, as did the prophet Nehemiah, refusing to allow schisms and isms to prevent her from being the woman God has created her to be, the woman who believes that all people are created in the image of God and are loved by God without conditions.

The Phoenix – Rising from the Ashes is her first completed work. She has already begun the sequel to this book, and is also working on two other books called Faces Behind the Pulpit, and The Fourth Generation: Curse of the Libido. In the past few years, Dian has discovered an interest in writing poetry and is adding that dream to her list of desires. She hopes that the messages in her books will reach those who desire to be empowered to live life to the fullest, without the shackles of bondage imposed by the institutional church or any faith tradition that would enslave any of God's creation.

Reverend Dian Griffin Jackson is happy to come to your area to speak, sing, or share her personal story with you. It is her desire to inspire women and men all over the world for indeed, God has still more to say, and She is saying it through this powerful little woman!